CalTPA Preparation Guide

Lynda R. Williams, Lecturer
Utah Valley University

Andrea M. Guillaume, Professor
California State University, Fullerton

Jennifer M. Ponder, Assistant Professor
California State University, Fullerton

PEARSON

Boston   Columbus   Indianapolis   New York   San Francisco   Upper Saddle River
Amsterdam   Cape Town   Dubai   London   Madrid   Milan   Munich   Paris   Montréal   Toronto
Delhi   Mexico City   São Paulo   Sydney   Hong Kong   Seoul   Singapore   Taipei   Tokyo

Vice President and Editorial Director:
 Jefferey W. Johnston
Vice President and Publisher: Kevin Davis
Editorial Assistant: Lauren Carlson
Vice President, Director of Marketing:
 Margaret Waples
Marketing Manager: Joanna Sabella
Senior Managing Editor: Pamela D. Bennett
Production Editor: Mary M. Irvin

Production Manager: Laura Messerly
Art Director: Jayne Conte
Cover Designer: Bruce Kenselaar
Cover Art: Fotolia
Project Coordination: Papitha Ramesh
Composition: Element LLC
Printer/Binder: Edwards Brothers
Cover Printer: Lehigh-Phoenix Color Corp.
Text Font: Palatino, 12/14

Credits and acknowledgments for materials borrowed from other sources and reproduced, with permission, in this textbook appear on the appropriate page within the text.

Every effort has been made to provide accurate and current Internet information in this book. However, the Internet and information posted on it are constantly changing, so it is inevitable that some of the Internet addresses listed in this textbook will change.

Library of Congress Cataloging-in-Publication Data
Williams, Lynda R.
  CalTPA preparation guide / Lynda R. Williams, Andrea M. Guillaume, Jennifer M. Ponder.
    p. cm.
  Includes bibliographical references and index.
  ISBN-13: 978-0-13-802177-1
  ISBN-10: 0-13-802177-5
  1. Teachers—California—Examinations—Study guides. 2. Teachers—Certification—
California. I. Guillaume, Andrea M. II. Ponder, Jennifer M. III. Title.
  LB1763.C2W55 2013
  371.1209794—dc23

                                                                                                              2011037131

10 9 8 7 6 5 4 3 2 1

ISBN 10:   0-13-802177-5
ISBN 13: 978-0-13-802177-1

CONTENTS

CalTPA Tips and You Try It! Features

Chapter	CalTPA Tips	You Try It!
Introduction: What Is the CalTPA? What Can the CalTPA Do for You?	• Travel Documents • Smoothing the Road to Submission	• Here's What I'm Thinking So Far CalTPA Quiz • Say This . . . Not That
PART 1: SKILLS FOR CALTPA SUCCESS		
Chapter 1: Understanding the Rubrics	• Format and Function	• Fill in the Blanks • Keep Your Story Straight
Chapter 2: Understanding CalTPA Vocabulary	• Word Caution • Vocabulary and Language Troubleshooting	• CalTPA Vocabulary Self-Rating • You Complete Me!
Chapter 3: Choosing Appropriate Focus Students	• Different Task = Different Focus Students • Attend to Terms Related to Focus Students	• Focus Student Criteria
Chapter 4: Preparing your CalTPA Responses: Important Tips and Reminders	• They Can Only Assess What You Write Down • Choose Your Words Carefully • Analyze Style Requirements • The Audience Matters	• Acceptable or Not? • Addressing the Prompt • Get Specific! • If the Shoe Fits . . . • Analytical or Descriptive? • Teacher as Artist
PART 2: MAKING ADAPTATIONS		
Chapter 5: Making Adaptations for English Learners	• Showcasing Your Skills at Providing Appropriate EL Adaptations • What? No CELDT Score? • English Language Development Standards • Build It Right or Fix It Later? • Avoiding Pitfalls: You're the Boss!	• Appropriate Practices for English Learners: Thumbs Up or Down? • Survivor: Voting EL Adaptations off the Island
Chapter 6: Making Adaptations for Learners with Special Needs	• Specifying UDL • Surfing the Net to Differentiate for Gifted Students • Invite Students to Reach for the Stars • Showcasing Your Skills in Adapting Instruction for Students With Special Needs • Check Your Adaptations	• Looking Back • Thumb Up or Thumbs Down: Appropriate Adaptations for Learners With Special Needs • Providing a Clear Rationale

ACKNOWLEDGMENTS

The authors wish to thank the following reviewers: Ann Palmer Bradley, Azusa Pacific University; Samuel Burke, Los Angeles Unified School District; Michael Cosenza, California Lutheran University; Nedra Crow, National University; Michael Madrid, Chapman University; Beverly Palley, Alliant International University; Stacy Schmidt, California State University–Bakersfield; Joy Springer, Pepperdine University; and Judy Washburn, California State University–Los Angeles.

INTRODUCTION

"I don't get stressed. I get prepared."
—Francesca, Middle School Teacher

Welcome to the part of your professional journey called the CalTPA (California Teaching Performance Assessment)! The CalTPA assesses your knowledge, skills, and abilities to teach the children of California's public schools. By passing the CalTPA, you demonstrate that you are prepared to help our students succeed.

Are you prepared for the CalTPA? This prep guide is an important tool to help you efficiently and effectively gain competence for the CalTPA. The following sections in this introduction provide an overview of the CalTPA, its related procedures, and suggestions for using this guide:

- What Is the CalTPA?
- It's the Law!
- Administration and Scoring of the CalTPA
- What If I Fail?
- What Can the CalTPA Do for Me?
- How Can This Prep Guide Help Me Survive and Thrive With the CalTPA?

WHAT IS THE CalTPA?

The CalTPA is a performance assessment composed of a series of four tasks, which are covered throughout your credential program. The CalTPA tasks are:

1. Subject Specific Pedagogy
2. Designing Instruction
3. Assessing Learning
4. Culminating Teaching Experience

Just as our K–12 students are expected to demonstrate mastery of core curriculum content standards through a series of assessments, so too are you required to master a set of outcomes. Your credential program is designed to provide you with opportunities to master the Teaching Performance Expectations (TPEs), which are considered imperative for new California teachers. Your program also incorporates a number of ways to ensure that you have mastered these TPEs. The CalTPA provides one more measure of your knowledge and skills related to twelve of the thirteen TPEs, as follows:

- TPE 1: Specific Pedagogical Skills for Subject Matter Instruction
- TPE 2: Monitoring Student Learning During Instruction
- TPE 3: Interpretation and Use of Assessments
- TPE 4: Making Content Accessible
- TPE 5: Student Engagement

- TPE 6: Developmentally Appropriate Teaching Practices
- TPE 7: Teaching English Learners
- TPE 8: Learning About Students
- TPE 9: Instructional Planning
- TPE 10: Instructional Time
- TPE 11: Social Environment
- TPE 13: Professional Growth

Each of the four CalTPA tasks assesses components of the TPEs so that, over time, you demonstrate your competence in the TPEs several times in different settings. The CalTPA builds in complexity and sophistication across the tasks. The tasks require you to work with actual students in cycles of planning, implementation (in the third and fourth tasks), and reflection. Unlike a multiple choice exam, the CalTPA is designed to assess your knowledge and skills in context. The tasks are things that competent teachers do daily: considering student needs and their implications, planning lessons, assessing student progress, and reflecting on effectiveness of lessons.

IT'S THE LAW!

Although California's credential programs have always required a competency check before recommending candidates for the credential, as of July 2008, state law (Senate Bill 2042 [Chapter 548, Statutes of 1998] and Senate Bill 1209 [Chapter 517, Statutes of 2006]) requires that candidates for the preliminary Multiple Subject and Single Subject credentials demonstrate competence through a Teaching Performance Assessment, or TPA. The law allows credential programs to develop their own TPA or to implement an approved model of the TPA. CalTPA is one of a few currently approved TPA models; your credential program chose to adopt it. Thus, for you, the CalTPA is a requirement for your preliminary credential. This prep guide is one important tool to assist you in completing the CalTPA. See *CalTPA Tip: Travel Documents* for other resources that will be important to you throughout your journey.

CalTPA Tip	
Travel Documents	
You will be accessing these materials throughout your CalTPA completion. Bookmark them or mark them as favorites in your web browser.	
Site	**Description and Purpose**
Teaching Performance Expectations http://www.ctc.ca.gov/educator-prep/TPA-files/TPEs-Full-Version.pdf	This document gives the full text of all thirteen TPEs. Be sure to review the relevant TPEs before you begin each CalTPA task.
TPA http://www.ctc.ca.gov/educator-prep/TPA.html	This page on the California Commission on Teacher Credentialing (CTC) website provides information on all models of the TPA.

CalTPA Teacher Candidate Information
http://www.ctc.ca.gov/educator-prep/TPA-California-candidates.html

This page includes specific information for each task, including rubrics and templates. You will download templates and enter your responses directly into them. This page also includes the Candidate Handbook. Download it and save it to your hard drive or print out a copy.

Standards and Frameworks
http://www.cde.ca.gov/be/st/

This page of the California Department of Education's site leads you to the approved student content standards and frameworks you will be using for each CalTPA task.

ADMINISTRATION AND SCORING OF THE CalTPA

The CalTPA tasks are typically completed in order in a timeframe specified by the credential program. You receive your scores on tasks as they are assessed, and your scores provide you and your program leader with ongoing information about your knowledge and skills. The CalTPA is public and open, meaning that anyone can access it on the Internet (the URL is found in *CalTPA Tip: Travel Documents*). The tasks themselves are a series of prompts; you insert your responses directly into a document template, which you save and later submit to your program for scoring. Thus, you have some flexibility as to when you complete the CalTPA, in accordance with your program's guidelines and schedules. See *CalTPA*

CalTPA Tip

Smoothing the Road to Submission

You want to focus on the content of your CalTPA responses to ensure that they clearly demonstrate your knowledge, skills, and abilities. To avoid technical issues that might interfere with your successful and timely CalTPA submission, try these tips:

- If you have a documented learning need, such as a learning disability, discuss it with the CalTPA contact person in your credential program before you begin your CalTPA responses. Depending on the issue, you may be allowed more time or different conditions for completing the CalTPA. PProgram personnel can't adapt for your needs if they don't know what your needs are. Advocate for yourself.
- Download all CalTPA materials directly from the CTC website. Only that site has the most current information.
- Save your files to a reliable hard drive. USB drives (flash drives, thumb drives, memory sticks) can be unstable. Back up your files.

> - Give files distinct names, perhaps including the dates you work on them, to ensure that you don't save old versions over new ones.
> - Double-check your program's requirements for naming files upon submission and for uploading documents.
> - For electronic submission, be sure that you will have a reliable Internet connection when you need it—before the submission date.
> - Check your tech supplies in advance. The fourth task requires parent permission forms and a video recording of your instruction. Do you have access to a scanner if you must submit permission forms electronically? Are you adept at using it? Do you have access to a video camera? Can you save, compress, and access video files? Build your tech skills now. Plan now to avoid tech emergencies later.

Tip: Smoothing the Road to Submission to ease issues of access, completion, storage, and submission.

The CalTPA is meant to measure your knowledge, skills, and abilities as an individual, so despite the fact that the assessment is publicly available, you are not allowed discuss your specific responses with others or receive assistance on any response you submit. Your CalTPA work is to be unaided. When directed to do so, you submit your responses to your credential program—not to the state. Most programs require electronic submission; some require paper back-up copies. Check with your program about specific submission requirements.

Your CalTPA responses will be scored by trained assessors who do not have access to your name. Assessors might include practicing teachers, faculty members, support providers, district personnel, or other education professionals. All assessors undergo training to certify them as scorers; they learn to eliminate personal biases and to assess your responses according to task-specific rubrics. The assessors periodically undergo recalibration to ensure that they continue to score responses fairly and consistently. Programs must double-score a minimum of 15 percent of responses each year to ensure reliability (consistency) in scoring. Scoring procedures are rubric-based and are designed to ensure that your work is assessed fairly.

As they analyze a response, assessors keep a Record of Evidence (ROE) where they note evidence of the knowledge and skills conveyed in the response. Each task is assessed holistically against the rubric and is awarded a score of 1, 2, 3, or 4. (Scoring rubrics are addressed in *Chapter 1: Understanding the Rubrics*.) To pass, you must receive a minimum score of 2 for each task and a minimum total of 12 across the four tasks. For example, you might earn a score of 3 on all four tasks for a combined score of 12, or you might earn a score of 2 on two tasks (that's 4 points) and a score of 4 on the other two tasks (that's 8 points) for a total of 12 points. However, credential programs are allowed to set higher passing standards. Many programs, for instance, require a score of 3 on each task. Check with your program for the scores that constitute a passing score.

WHAT IF I FAIL?

California's credential programs are accredited and work hard to prepare candidates well—for the classroom and for the TPA. CalTPA first-try pass rates can approach 90 percent. So rest assured that many candidates pass all four tasks on their first try. Still, thinking about the possibility of failing.; and prompting a little anxiety can be a healthy motivator.

However, if you fail one or more CalTPA tasks on the first try, you will get another chance. Your program is required to provide one additional opportunity to retake the failed task(s). Some programs allow two retakes per task. Check with your credential program for the local policy.

If you resubmit a task, a trained person will do remediation to help you prepare for the next submission. The person doing remediation will have access to your Record of Evidence before meeting with you. Remediation focuses on helping you understand the task and its demands, based on patterns in your earlier performance. The condition that your work remain unaided still holds.

The reasons some candidates fail one or more CalTPA tasks are varied. Some candidates need more time or additional opportunities to master the TPEs and satisfactorily demonstrate knowledge, skills, and abilities. However, some candidates fail because they procrastinate, do not understand the demands of the tasks, or do not follow the instructions carefully. That's where this prep guide can help! By reading this far, you've already taken steps in the right direction to ensure that, through your CalTPA responses, you maximize your opportunities to demonstrate your knowledge and abilities as a new California public school teacher. Check your CalTPA knowledge in the *You Try It! Here's What I'm Thinking So Far CalTPA Quiz*. This quiz is the first of many Try It! activities you'll encounter in this guide.

You Try It!

Here's What I'm Thinking So Far
CalTPA Quiz

Active readers check their comprehension and revisit the text to make sure they understand and can apply what they are reading. Read each statement and determine if it is true or false. Circle T or F, then check your work in the Appendix.

1. Teaching Performance Assessments (like the CalTPA) are mandated by federal legislation, the No Child Left Behind Act, which requires well-prepared teachers for every student.   T   F

2. The CalTPA is an objective exam taken in a secure location upon completion of the credential program.   T   F

3. The CalTPA measures your knowledge, skills, and abilities related to all thirteen Teaching Performance Expectations.   T   F

4. The CalTPA has four sections, or tasks.   T   F

5. A candidate who fails a portion of the CalTPA on the first try can retake it.   T   F

WHAT CAN THE CalTPA DO FOR ME?

The CalTPA is not "just one more thing" you need to do in your credential program. It is important work that will help you succeed as a teacher. The CalTPA addresses four stated purposes (California Commission on Teacher Credentialing, 2009).

1. *Formative information for you as a credential candidate.* Formative means that the experience can help shape—or form—your future choices about what you need to learn and how you might go about learning it. Each task will give you an overall score of your knowledge and skills from a trained, impartial assessor; the score provides you with an opportunity for self-analysis and reflection on what you know and need to learn next. Good teachers never stop learning.

2. *Summative—or summary—information that allows your institution to recommend you for the credential.* The fact that all new teachers pass a rigorous assessment can add to the public's confidence that our teachers are prepared for California's classrooms.

3. *Information about the effectiveness of your credential program.* As your program personnel study CalTPA scoring patterns (required by their accreditation process), they can improve the program for the next credential candidates.

4. *Information for the next phase of your professional development, induction.* After you complete your preliminary credential and take a classroom teaching position, you will begin work to clear your credential. Most new teachers do so through induction programs that build on the considerable knowledge and skills you have attained through your preliminary credential program. Although privacy laws prohibit programs from requiring you to share your CalTPA scores or experiences, you may choose to do so as you and your induction program leaders devise a plan for the next phase of your professional growth.

There is no escaping the fact that the CalTPA is a high-stakes assessment. You must pass it in order to receive your credential. We encourage you to embrace the notion that, by becoming a teacher, you are joining *a profession.* In a profession, specially educated people share a language and body of knowledge; they agree to a set of principles, ethical standards, and policies that govern their behavior and hold them accountable to their constituents and the public.

By using an assessment as a condition of credentialing, California's teaching profession joins many professions in requiring tests or other assessments for licensure. In the United States, professionals who require assessments for licensure include, for example, physicians, attorneys, accountants, pharmacists, psychologists, architects, and engineers. We, the public, *deserve* the assurance that our attorneys, our psychologists, and our engineers have demonstrated their competence before receiving licenses to practice. California expects nothing less from its teachers.

We hope we have convinced you that a Teaching Performance Assessment has benefits as a mark of entrance to the education profession . Thus, we encourage you to adopt a positive stance as you face your CalTPA responsibility and invest your time in completing the tasks.

You Try It!

Get Specific!

CalTPA tasks, like CTE, ask you to describe what you learn about your students' health considerations and describe how you will use this information in planning academic instruction.

Here are three general statements a candidate wrote in response to that prompt. Get specific. Expand each statement to include more detail. Check our sample in the Appendix.

- Some of my students are overweight.

- Other students have food allergies.

- My lessons will incorporate this information.

---

passed the test." Instead, provide the work samples or test results along with the data you have collected and explain your interpretations of evidence and conclusions.

You Try It!

If the Shoe Fits . . .

Which paragraph is an example of descriptive writing? Which is an example of analytical writing? Write A or D on the line to identify the writing style. See the Appendix for our answers.

1. The old pair of grey running shoes was slightly worn with soft edges and scuffs on the toes. The laces were frayed on the ends and the shoes no longer made a squeaking sound as they moved along the hardwood floor. A stale scent reminiscent of the gym lingered in the air surrounding the comfortable but dirty shoes. _____

2. This particular pair of shoes was built with 60 percent more padding in the heel to allow the runner to hit their stride in comfort. The manufacturer built the shoe with just enough support in the arch, while still maintaining the flexibility runners need to bend their foot in comfort. In a survey of 100 people who wore these shoes for running three times a week for two months, 90 percent of the respondents felt that the shoes gave them adequate support for both their feet and ankles and helped them to reach their peak performance. _____

3. Now imagine this was the prompt for the above responses. **How will these shoes benefit the runner?** Which response (1 or 2) would be the more appropriate response? _____

In sum, it's critical that you identify the type of writing required of you at different points in the CalTPA. Providing a descriptive response when an analytical one is required is likely to cause assessors to judge your work as *cursory, limited, minimal,* or *vague* (Score Level 2 descrip-

---

You Try It!

Analytical or Descriptive?

Which prompts are asking for analytical writing? Which are asking for descriptive writing? Write A next to the item if it requires an analytical response (including reflective). Write D next to the item if it requires a descriptive response. Check the Appendix for our answers.

1. Was the implementation and timing of this assessment appropriate for this class? Why? _____

2. If you were given an opportunity to use the assessment again, what part(s) would you keep and what part(s) might you change? Why? _____

3. Describe other information relevant to this academic content area that you learned about the student (e.g., attendance, extracurricular activities)._____

4. What is (are) your academic learning goal(s)? What specifically do you expect students to know or be able to do as a result of the lesson?_____

5. How will you use what you have learned regarding connecting instructional planning to student characteristics in the future?_____

---

tors) rather than as *convincing* and *compelling.* Try the *You Try It! If the Shoe Fits . . .* to practice distinguishing between descriptive and analytical writing.

Reflection Self-Analysis

Three of the four CalTPA tasks (all but Subject Specific Pedagogy) require reflection. Reflection is a special form of analytical writing; it's self-analysis. You reflect on your experiences in planning instruction and assessment and analyze how this information will affect future practice. Thinking about what you did, why you did it, what you learned, and how it will influence you in the future as a teacher will help you to set goals and consider alternatives to the educational decisions that you have made. For example, if you had the chance to teach this lesson again, what would you do differently and why? What would you keep the same? Effective reflective responses go beyond *cursory* surface level treatment of events and instead are *purposefully connected, reinforced,* and *compelling.* For more practice identifying the type of writing required, try the ***You Try It! Analytical or Descriptive?*** activity.

SHOWCASING: CLEARLY DEMONSTRATING YOUR KNOWLEDGE AND SKILLS

To showcase your knowledge and skills, aim for the highest score and you can feel more confident that, even if you don't achieve that target, your response will be a competent Score Level 3. The amount of detail

---

You Try It!

Teacher as Artist

Envision yourself as an artist creating a masterpiece. As a masterpiece, your work will of course exhibit the highest standards in the discipline. However, it will also convey a sense of you as an artist. Each CalTPA task is a blank canvas. You must choose the tools, techniques, and style to express yourself while simultaneously conveying your knowledge and skills. What tools will you use to create your work of art? Think about the style you want to use to express yourself. The decisions you make will impact the final product.

As you select your style, remember, too, that some styles are better than others for conveying a clear, unequivocal message to the audience, your assessor. For practice, search the Internet for examples of the two painting styles referenced in the following. Circle a or b: Which style of art should be a metaphor for your CalTPA responses?

Example a.   Abstract: *Moon Woman* by Jackson Pollack

Abstract —   *A style of art that does not show the exact details of people, places, or objects as observed in real life. An abstract image is evocative rather than purely representational.*

Example b.   Realism: *Mona Lisa* by Leonardo Da Vinci

Realism —   *A style of art that shows the exact characteristics of people, places, or objects.*

---

and the depth of your responses will determine whether or not you pass each individual task, and they will also be the deciding factor between a Score Level 4 or 3. The following sections explain how you can clearly demonstrate your knowledge and skills in each CalTPA task.

CalTPA TIP

The Audience Matters

Treat each CalTPA task as a mock interview for a teaching position. Impress your audience with your strong understanding of the skills needed for effective teaching. Imagine that Joe or Josephine Assessor is at your CalTPA "interview" and keep him or her in mind as you compose your responses. You want that job!

What Does It Mean to Showcase Your Skills?

As a verb, *showcase* means "to show to best advantage." Your CalTPA responses should clearly demonstrate your knowledge, skills, and abilities. When you studied the CalTPA rubrics in *Chapter 1: Understanding the Rubrics*, you discovered that Score Level 4 responses are *clear, specific, relevant, accurate,* and *detailed*. They *convince* the assessor of the candidate's knowledge and skills. Your rich stores of pedagogical knowledge are worth nothing on the CalTPA if your responses do not display that knowledge in clear, connected, and compelling ways to the assessor. Consider your responses for each CalTPA task as a personal showcase to exhibit your knowledge and skills. Use *You Try It! Teacher as Artist* both to think about your own style and to keep your audience clearly in mind as you write.

Did you circle *b*? We agree. For a high-stakes assessment where clarity is required and ambiguity is to be avoided, abstract styles are far too open to interpretation. Too many sets of inferences might be drawn from an "abstract" CalTPA response. Assessors might be able to see the world through your eyes, but then again, they might misinterpret your vision. A CalTPA response that is straightforward and does not require the assessor to make inferences is more likely to earn the critical praise (and high score) it deserves. The audience matters.

Top 10 List: Tips for Showcasing

Be strategic when planning your lesson and responses for each CalTPA task! Provide specific examples of subject specific pedagogy, active learning strategies, assessment tools, and modifications. Support your decisions with clear rationales. Use our Top 10 Tips to help you showcase your knowledge and skills in each response. These tips are restated in each task-specific chapter; consider how the specific suggestions and examples apply to your responses.

1. Get to know all the students in your class before you plan your lesson and select focus students. Learn about each student's individual and specific needs. Use multiple sources to collect data about the students' linguistic, physical, social, cultural, and emotional needs.
2. Connect the information you learn about the students to your specific lesson and content area for each task. Show the assessors that you are actually using what you learn about students to plan your instruction.
3. Think carefully before you select your two focus students. Select focus students who allow you to demonstrate your ability to make appropriate adaptations.
4. Plan instruction that can be specifically adapted for each focus student.
5. Make explicit connections to classroom coursework, readings, and materials to support your instructional decisions. For example, it is not enough to say that you will use visuals for your English learner. You must take it a step further and explain why a visual is appropriate for the English learner. Consider her level of English

proficiency, the strategies appropriate for her level, and specific *> not just CELDT...* readings, theories, or course materials that support those choices.

6. Organize your assessment data before you try to analyze it. You might consider using a spreadsheet or a checklist to track connections in responses.

7. Demonstrate that you have more than one tool in your tool box. Even if you feel that you chose the best instructional strategies, modifications, or assessment formats, remember that there is always more than one way to accomplish a goal. Prove to the assessors that you possess a wide range of knowledge and skills and can approach a lesson with different strategies. The analysis and reflection prompts are appropriate places to suggest alternative possibilities.

8. Pay attention to your writing style. Some sections call for descriptive writing, whereas other sections require analytical responses.

9. Make sure your responses are clear and concise. Even though you are not penalized for spelling and grammar, an edited response lets the assessor focus on your knowledge and skills rather than your ability to write.

10. Take the time to organize your response so the assessor can easily locate key information. You might consider using formatting tools such as headings, labels, underlining, bold text, or numbers to organize your response.

Chapter Summary

Because this chapter addressed diverse topics to ensure your CalTPA success, the summary is arranged by those topics.

Professional and Moral Obligations

Due to the stress associated with high-stakes assessments, some people are tempted to engage in activities that could have devastating consequences for their future career. Demonstrate integrity, honesty, and responsibility as a professional educator.

Reading and Following Instructions

Reading carefully, following directions, and addressing the prompts fully will help you successfully complete the four CalTPA tasks. Giving detailed and complete responses that directly address the prompt is the best way to demonstrate your skills and knowledge.

Writing Styles

The CalTPA requires you to write effectively using both descriptive and analytical writing.

Use descriptive writing to answer the *what* and *which* questions. Use analytical writing when asked to explain *how, why,* or *in what way.* Both styles of writing will help you write responses that give the assessor a clear picture of your class, your choices, and your understanding of what it means to be an effective teacher.

Showcasing: Clearly Demonstrating Your Knowledge and Skills

Take the extra time to clearly organize your response and make purposeful connections to course content, readings, and discussions. A well-organized response will showcase your knowledge and skills by emphasizing key points. Treat the response writing as though you were interviewing for a position. Make yourself stand out from the other candidates. Use every exercise in this guide as a learning experience that will help you to further your professional growth and development.

PONDER THIS...

- You have learned a great deal in your credential program. You are ready to demonstrate your extensive knowledge and skills on the CalTPA. What steps can you take to make sure that you follow a code of ethics?
- Think about the next CalTPA task you will complete. What will you do first? Why?
- How does information in this chapter about writing styles connect with information about reading and following directions?
- Think back to your past professional successes. What have others told you are your particular strengths and skills? What makes you shine? How can you incorporate your past successes in showcasing your skills during the CalTPA?

2

Making Adaptations

5

■ ■ ■

Making Adaptations for English Learners

"I didn't know it could be like this!"

—XOCHITL, A SECOND-GRADER AND AN EARLY
INTERMEDIATE ENGLISH LEARNER, AS SHE EXCITEDLY
TESTED DIFFERENT MATERIALS IN THE CLASSROOM FOR
THEIR ELECTRICAL CONDUCTIVITY

Across the United States, approximately 11 percent of K–12 students are English learners (NCES, 2007–08), but in California, more than 25 percent of our students are English learners* (Watanabe, 2010). That's more than 1.6 million students. In fact, California has more English learners than the average state has students (NCES, 2010). English learners need special, systematic support to ensure that they can meet rigorous content standards while they acquire English. Your credential program is required to prepare you to work with English learners, and each of the four CalTPA tasks explicitly requires you to consider the needs of English learners. This chapter prepares you to consider adaptations to instruction and assessment for your English learners across the CalTPA. It is organized in the following sections:

- Laws Pertaining to English Learners
- California English Language Development Test (CELDT)
- Principles and Strategies for Instructing English Learners
- Differentiated Support for English Learners
- Assessing English Learners

---

*Other terms for English learners you may see include English language learners (ELL) and Limited English Proficient (LEP) students. The California Department of Education (2006) defines an English learner as, "a K–12 student who, based on objective assessment, has not developed listening, speaking, reading, and writing proficiencies in English sufficient for participation in the regular school program" (p. 2).

LAWS PERTAINING TO ENGLISH LEARNERS

Laws at many levels present the rights of English learners and stipulate how they should be educated. Here are five key laws and decisions at both the federal and state level.

1. *Title VI of the Civil Rights Act of 1964* prohibits discrimination on the basis of national origin, race, or color. It requires that programs for English learners be based on sound theory, receive adequate support, and undergo review and revision.
2. *Lau v. Nichols* (1970) requires school districts to take steps to help English learners to overcome language barriers and to ensure their meaningful participation in districts' educational programs. (Read a summary of the decision at http://www.law.cornell.edu/supct/html/historics/USSC_CR_0414_0563_ZO.html.)
3. *No Child Left Behind Act of 2001* has two titles that pertain to English learners. Title I mandates that English learners be given the opportunities to master grade-level state standards, be assessed yearly, and have achievement scores reported as a subgroup. Title III provides funding to school agencies to help increase English proficiency and content knowledge for English learners, requires that programs for meeting their needs have a scientific base, and requires parent communication regarding students' language assessment and educational programs.
4. *California Education Code Sections 300–340* formalize Proposition 227, passed by the people of California in 1998. Section 305 specifies that, in California public schools, all children be taught in English. It mandates that all students be placed in English classrooms. English learners may be taught through sheltered English immersion for the period of one year. Family members may complete a waiver to have their students educated in bilingual settings. (Read the law yourself at *http://www.leginfo.ca.gov/calaw.html.* Section 305 is found at *http://www.leginfo.ca.gov/cgi-bin/displaycode?section=edc&group=00001-01000&file=305-306.*) Sections 306 and 310 mandate that instruction in English language classrooms must be overwhelmingly in English. In structured English immersion classrooms, instruction must be nearly all in English and districts must determine allowable percentages of instruction to be provided in the students' primary language.
5. *California Education Code Section 44253.1* recognizes the right of English learners to receive a quality education and thus requires that teachers have the knowledge and skills to teach English language development and specially designed content instruction in English.

In general, these laws and decisions stress the importance of fair and appropriate support for K–12 students as they acquire English, now most often in an English-speaking classroom. Be sure to check with your school district's local policies regarding English learners too.

CALIFORNIA ENGLISH LANGUAGE DEVELOPMENT TEST (CELDT)

Both state law and the No Child Left Behind Act require the initial and annual testing of English learners' English development. In California, we use the California English Language Development Test (CELDT). The purpose of the CELDT is to identify the English learners' levels of English development and to monitor their English language progress. The CELDT assesses K–12 English learners' listening and speaking, reading, and writing skills. Students may not opt out of the test. The test takes about two hours and is administered by a trained district person who is fully fluent in English. Students take the test annually until they are reclassified as Fluent English Proficient.

Based on their performance, English learners are identified as being at one of five English performance levels. The five performance levels identified by the CELDT are Beginning, Early Intermediate, Intermediate, Early Advanced, and Advanced (Levels 1–5). These levels are described later in this chapter.

CalTPA Tip

Showcasing Your Skills at Providing Appropriate EL Adaptations

Because the CalTPA measures your ability to adapt instruction for English learners, choose students who require many adaptations. If you have an option, choose a student at a lower level of English proficiency. Adaptations for the advanced English learner are often more subtle and less obvious than are adaptations for beginning speakers.

You can read more about the CELDT, see released questions, and see CELDT scores at the Testing and Accountability pages of the Department of Education's site (www.cde.gov and specifically at DataQuest [http://dq.cde.ca.gov/dataquest/]). In 2010–2011, two-thirds of the students who took the CELDT scored as Intermediate or Early Advanced. Knowing students' CELDT scores can help you adapt your instruction to maximize their English language development and their content mastery. See the *CalTPA Tip: What? No CELDT Score?* for more ideas on estimating students' English language levels.

GENERAL PRINCIPLES FOR APPROPRIATE INSTRUCTION FOR ENGLISH LEARNERS

CalTPA tasks Subject Specific Pedagogy, Designing Instruction, and Culminating Teaching Experience all require you to plan instruction that addresses two goals for English learner success: English language development and content mastery. View every lesson as an opportunity to help your English learners develop and practice new skills in the English

CalTPA Tip

What? No CELDT Score?

Sometimes CELDT scores may be unavailable. For example, your English learner focus student may have just arrived, testing for the year may not have occurred, or scores may be pending. In the absence of CELDT scores, rely on other information sources for estimating the student's level of English proficiency.

- Interview the student.
- Listen to the student's spoken language in informal settings.
- Listen to the student use English in a variety of academic contexts such as partner talk, small-group work, and in front of the class. Remember that speaking before a large group of people is stressful; stress can affect language usage.
- Examine the student's written language.
- Talk with the student's parents, either in English, the home language, or through an interpreter.
- If you have a master teacher, ask for advice.
- Interview other teachers or personnel who know the student.
- Check student records.

In your CalTPA response, state explicitly that you have estimated the English language level based on a number of sources until CELDT scores become available.

language. See *CalTPA Tip: English Language Development Standards*. Also ensure that you are employing strategies that will help English learners master grade-level academic content.

CalTPA Tip

English Language Development Standards

In addition to the content standards in a variety of subjects, California has standards for English language development (ELD). The ELD standards specify the reading, writing, listening, and speaking expectations for K–12 students who are acquiring English. Check to ensure that your CalTPA lessons are appropriate for your focus students' ELD standard expectations. Review the ELD standards at the Department of Education's website (http://www.cde.ca.gov/BE/ST/SS/index.asp).

Five general principles will help you facilitate English language development and content mastery for all of your English learners (Center for Research on Education, Diversity & Excellence, 2002; Cummins, 1981; Echevarria, Vogt & Short, 2010a, 2010b; Fillmore & Snow, 2000; Gersten et al., 2007; Hill & Flynn, 2006; Krashen, 1981; Meyer, 2000; Swain, 1985;

Thomas & Collier, 2001). Here are the principles for English learners' success:

1. Build a supportive environment.
   • Use classroom routines and provide an orderly learning environment.
   • Learn about students and incorporate their cultures and interests.
   • Use culturally relevant examples.
   • Focus on communication and help students feel free to take risks as they practice their language.

2. Keep a clear focus on the content and on language development.
   • Choose content carefully; focus on developing key ideas well.
   • State the objective.
   • Connect to prior knowledge.
   • Explicitly teach vocabulary for basic communication and for academic English.
   • Teach vocabulary well by focusing on meaningful development, varied instruction, and multiple opportunities to practice.
   • Teach English sentence structures, grammar, and idioms.
   • Preview/review.
   • Check for understanding.
   • Focus on higher-level thinking and teach learning strategies.
   • Maximize student engagement with the content.

3. Provide a rich learning environment.
   • Embed content in meaningful contexts.
   • Connect content to real-life and prior experiences.
   • Create a print-rich environment.
   • Use real objects (realia) and manipulatives.
   • Use pictures and video.
   • Employ digital technologies.
   • Use guest speakers and field trips.
   • Provide input that is kinesthetic, linguistic, organizational, and visual.

4. Make your input comprehensible.
   • Use caregiver speech. Think of how parents talk with children as they learn their first language and adopt some of those patterns, as appropriate for your student's age and development. Examples include simpler nouns, exaggerated intonation, and a focus on the "here and now" so the context provides clear hints about meaning,
   • Simplify speech. Slow down, use fewer figures of speech, use repetition, and use gestures to clarify meaning.
   • Use multiple forms of input. Don't just say directions aloud; put them on a chart that includes both words and drawings.
   • Simplify text. For example, provide outlines, highlight passages, rewrite it, or use materials adapted for different readability levels.
   • Provide primary language support (e.g., texts in the native language) as appropriate.
   • Use computer-based technologies, perhaps in the primary language.

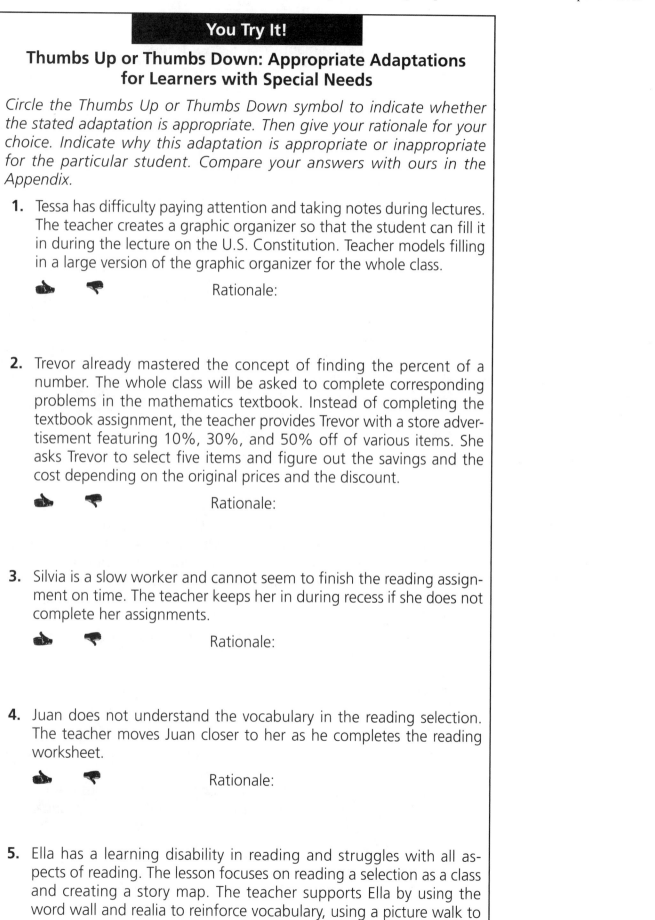

You Try It!

Thumbs Up or Thumbs Down: Appropriate Adaptations for Learners with Special Needs

Circle the Thumbs Up or Thumbs Down symbol to indicate whether the stated adaptation is appropriate. Then give your rationale for your choice. Indicate why this adaptation is appropriate or inappropriate for the particular student. Compare your answers with ours in the Appendix.

1. Tessa has difficulty paying attention and taking notes during lectures. The teacher creates a graphic organizer so that the student can fill it in during the lecture on the U.S. Constitution. Teacher models filling in a large version of the graphic organizer for the whole class.

   👍 👎   Rationale:

2. Trevor already mastered the concept of finding the percent of a number. The whole class will be asked to complete corresponding problems in the mathematics textbook. Instead of completing the textbook assignment, the teacher provides Trevor with a store advertisement featuring 10%, 30%, and 50% off of various items. She asks Trevor to select five items and figure out the savings and the cost depending on the original prices and the discount.

   👍 👎   Rationale:

3. Silvia is a slow worker and cannot seem to finish the reading assignment on time. The teacher keeps her in during recess if she does not complete her assignments.

   👍 👎   Rationale:

4. Juan does not understand the vocabulary in the reading selection. The teacher moves Juan closer to her as he completes the reading worksheet.

   👍 👎   Rationale:

5. Ella has a learning disability in reading and struggles with all aspects of reading. The lesson focuses on reading a selection as a class and creating a story map. The teacher supports Ella by using the word wall and realia to reinforce vocabulary, using a picture walk to

introduce the story, asking comprehension questions, reading as a class, and creating a giant story map as a class.

    Rationale:

6. Wesley is bright and works ahead of the class. The teacher is planning a lesson that he knows Wesley has already mastered. The teacher gives Wesley extra worksheets and lets him help the other students who do not understand the concept.

    Rationale:

7. Meggie is a selective mute due to some early emotional trauma. She does not verbalize her understanding easily or willingly. The teacher has an assessment planned that is a one-on-one interview, but the teacher knows Meggie will probably not respond. The IEP in place suggests assessing Meggie by alternative means. The teacher decides to allow Maggie to use a combination of gestures and pointing to the correct answer and written responses that will allow her to express herself without speaking.

Rationale:

8. The biology teacher requires students to keep a three-ring binder with multiple sections, all pages numbered and listed in a table of contents. She assesses students' notebooks by giving them thirty seconds to find pages she calls out in advance. Organization is a strong need for Dan, and he takes longer than others to read. Although he keeps his biology notebook up-to-date, he cannot find the pages quickly. To adapt, the teacher allows Dan to return at study hall and show her his notebook.

Rationale:

9. The geometry teacher knows that Kara has difficulty keeping up with lectures. Kara also needs to hear the information more than once to really understand it. The geometry teacher does not feel it is right to slow down the lesson for one student, so he has one of the GATE students work with Kara, and he tells her to just try and keep up with the lectures as best as she can.

    Rationale:

PROVIDING A CLEAR AND COMPELLING RATIONALE

Chapter 4: Preparing Your CalTPA Responses: Important Tips and Reminders introduced you to the importance of using analytical writing on the CalTPA. When the CalTPA tasks ask you to adapt instruction for a variety of learner needs, you must provide a rationale—an analysis—of your adaptations. Recall from *Chapter 1: Understanding the Rubrics* that a Score Level 4 response *clearly, consistently,* and *convincingly* demonstrates *appropriate, accurate,* and *relevant* evidence of knowledge and skills in a manner that *connects evidence purposefully* and *reinforces* it across the response. Clearly, the rationales for the adaptations you describe in the CalTPA are crucial. To provide a strong rationale, ask yourself questions such as: Why is this adaptation appropriate? How will it help the student? Describe exactly how the chosen adaptation will benefit the student's assessed needs. Explain how the adaptation is appropriate both for content goals and for the student's individual development. Use *You Try It! Providing a Clear Rationale* to practice identifying effective adaptations and writing compelling rationales.

> Raitionale

You Try It!

Providing a Clear Rationale

Read the following two scenarios and choose the rationale that most clearly explains the need for the adaptation and how it will help the student. Check the key in the Appendix.

1. Jim is an eleventh-grade student with a hearing impairment. Jim's IEP requires that the teacher use a microphone and that Jim has the receiver near him. The teacher has also elected to record lectures for Jim to revisit later. The teacher will also provide visual aids in his lecture.
   a. I made this adaptation for Jim because that is what the IEP said to do. All students like visual aids.
   b. He needs to hear the lecture.
   c. Using the microphone will allow Jim to have equal access to all of the information presented because he will be able to hear everything that is going on. By recording the lectures, Jim will be able to review the information at his own pace and if he misses something due to his hearing deficit, he will have an opportunity to hear it again. Visual aids will provide information for Jim that is not dependent on his hearing ability.

2. Ava has difficulty in reading. She reads far below grade level. The fifth-grade teacher is planning a lesson to address the California state content standard *Discuss the experiences of settlers on the overland trails to the West.* She plans to have the students read information from primary sources (letters and journals from people on the overland trails). The students will be given a graphic organizer to fill out as they gather information from their reading. The

teacher has decided to provide Ava with some video and audio clips that will give her access to the same information. While the other students are reading the books, Ava will be seated at the computer with headphones. She will listen to the audio clips and watch the video clips and jot down information on the graphic organizer.

a. Ava will benefit from having alternative ways to gather information. She will be able to hear the primary sources read and watch video clips related to the topic without having to read something beyond her level.

b. The graphic organizer and website will keep Ava busy and keep her from slowing down the other students because of her reading level. It is unfair to the other students to constantly have to wait for Ava to read something. The graphic organizer will be collected. She will be turning in the same work as her peers.

c. Everyone got a graphic organizer, so there really was no need for an adaptation here.

Chapter Summary

Every student in your class can and will learn. As the teacher, you are responsible, legally and ethically, for providing appropriate adaptations based on your students' individual needs. As you move forward through the four CalTPA tasks, use the information in this chapter as a resource for making adaptations for students with special needs. The following resources can take you yet another step farther in your knowledge and skills in providing instruction that is appropriate for all students.

- Suite101.com: http://specialneedseducation.suite101.com/article.cfm/learning_disability_accommodations
- National Center for Learning Disabilities: http://www.ncld.org
- National Association for Gifted Children: http://www.nagc.org
- Center for Applied Special Technology *Universal Design for Learning:* http://www.cast.org/research/udl/index.html
- U.S. Department of Justice: *A Guide to Disability Rights Laws:* http://www.ada.gov/cguide.htm
- U.S. Department of Education: http://www.ed.gov/
- U.S. Department of Health and Human Services *Your Rights Under Section 504 of Rehabilitation Act:* http://www.hhs.gov/ocr/504.html
- LD online: http://www.ldonline.org
- The Iris Center: http://iris.peabody.vanderbilt.edu
- Learning Disabilities Association of America: http://www.ldanatl.org/

PONDER THIS...

The Individuals with Disabilities Education Act of 2004 states that you must use "person first" language. You should use terms like *students with learning disabilities* rather than LD students. Think about a student in your class who has a particular challenge to learning. How will you describe the student? What words will you use when you write about the student? How will you keep the student first?

Task Specific Support

7

■ ■ ■

Subject Specific Pedagogy

"It is the supreme art of the teacher to awaken joy in creative expression and knowledge."

—ALBERT EINSTEIN

Intending to create "supreme art," teachers employ *pedagogy*—the art of teaching—daily. *Pedagogy* also refers to instructional methods, strategies, and decisions employed by teachers. Through effective pedagogy, teachers match their knowledge of students to the demands of their subject matter to foster success. The first task of the CalTPA, Subject Specific Pedagogy (SSP), assesses your competence in planning and adapting instruction that is appropriate for students and for the subject matter. This chapter guides you through SSP by employing the following sections:

- Overview of the Subject Specific Pedagogy Task
- Getting to Know SSP's Four Case Studies
- Getting Specific: Case Study One
- Getting Specific: Case Study Two
- Getting Specific: Case Study Three
- Getting Specific: Case Study Four

OVERVIEW OF THE SUBJECT SPECIFIC PEDAGOGY TASK

Subject Specific Pedagogy is the least complex CalTPA task and is the only one that does not require candidates to choose focus students or plan instruction or assessment for a real class. Instead, it presents a series of four case studies, or scenarios, based on a specific content area and students whose characteristics match those authorized by the intended credential. Each case study is based on a set of state content standards; your task is to plan instruction, assessments, and adaptations that help students make progress toward these academic content standards. Check your knowledge about content standards using *You Try It! What Do You Know About Content Standards?*

You Try It!

What Do You Know About Content Standards?

Circle T (True) or F (False). Hint: Half of these statements are true. Check your answers in the Appendix.

1. T F Most content areas taught in K–12 public schools have adopted standards.

2. T F Content standards present discrete lists of topics.

3. T F Content standards are statements of things teachers should cover.

4. T F Content standards drive learning goals.

5. T F Content standards are all highly specific.

6. T F Content standards drive assessments.

Even though it contains four case studies the only one of the CalTPA tasks to be segmented so SSP yields a single score. You will receive one score (1, 2, 3, or 4) that represents your work across all four case studies.

In SSP, you demonstrate your knowledge of pedagogy that is content specific and developmentally appropriate. *Content-specific* means you will show the CalTPA scorers that you understand the kinds of instructional strategies that are appropriate for your subject area. Biology teachers employ strategies that match demands of science, for instance, and history teachers use strategies that fit well for history. *Developmentally appropriate* means that your responses, instructional plans, and assessments reflect an understanding of the needs and interests of students in the age range specified by your credential. Finally, in SSP, you will demonstrate your ability to adapt instruction for individual student needs, specifically for the needs of an English learner and of a learner with special needs. The SSP demonstrates your competence in six Teaching Performance Expectations:

- TPE 1: Specific Pedagogical Skills for Subject Matter Instruction
- TPE 3: Interpretation and Use of Assessments
- TPE 4: Making Content Accessible
- TPE 6: Developmentally Appropriate Teaching Practices
- TPE 7: Teaching English learners
- TPE 9: Instructional Planning

The TPEs are found on the Commission for Teacher Credentialing website (*http://www.ctc.ca.gov/educator-prep/TPA-California-candidates. html*), along with the task rubrics. We suggest that you review the task rubric before you begin a CalTPA task. Also consider reviewing *Chapter 1: Understanding the Rubrics.*

GETTING TO KNOW SSP'S FOUR CASE STUDIES

The four SSP cases are similar in structure. Each case study presents a scenario followed by a set of prompts. The similarities among the case studies end there. Each case presents a different classroom and has a different emphasis. Case Study 1 asks you to *plan instruction* that is developmentally appropriate and subject specific. Case Study 2 requires you to *analyze assessment practices*. Case Study 3 presents instruction and requires you to *adapt it for an English learner*, and Case Study 4 asks you to *adapt instruction for a student with special needs*.

There are other differences among the case studies. The content varies by case study. For Multiple Subject Credential candidates, cases address—in order—language arts, mathematics, science, and social studies. For Single Subject candidates, there are currently more than a dozen subject-specific versions of the SSP, and the content within each SSP varies to address different domains of the subject authorized by the credential. Finally, the student grade levels addressed in SSP also differ across the case studies for Multiple and Single Subject candidates.

Begin by gaining an overall sense of all of the case studies. Complete the chart in *You Try It! Charting the SSP*, as you read the SSP template. The Appendix presents a partially completed chart for the Single Subject SSP in Art.

	You Try It!			
	Charting the SSP			
	Case Study 1 Subject-Specific and Developmentally Appropriate Pedagogy	**Case Study 2** Assessment Practices	**Case Study 3** Adaptation of Subject-Specific Pedagogy for English Learners	**Case Study 4** Adaptation of Subject-Specific Pedagogy for Students with Special Needs
Grade Level and Subject Area				
Context *What are the setting and goals?* **People** *Who are the students? What are their needs?*				
Job *In one sentence, what are you asked to do?*				
Prompts *How many? What are they?*				

You Try It! Charting the SSP provides an overview of the four case studies and can also be an aid to help you avoid redundancy in your response. The *CalTPA Tip: Been There, Done That* provides suggestions on avoiding repetition in your CalTPA responses.

CalTPA Tip

Been There, Done That

Some candidates have felt that their CalTPA responses are redundant, remarking that they feel they have said the same thing more than once. These three suggestions can help you avoid that "Been There, Done That" feeling.

1. Recall that the CalTPA rubric for a Score Level 4 requires that evidence must be *purposefully connected and reinforced* across the response. A response that restates points can strengthen connections between ideas and reinforcing points.
2. Read the prompts again. Each prompt asks for unique—not redundant—information. Ask yourself how one prompt is different from the next. If they look identical, you are probably missing something specific in the prompt.
3. Avoid repetition from the start by reading all prompts before you begin. This will help you to avoid prematurely addressing a future prompt.

GETTING SPECIFIC: CASE STUDY 1

Case Study 1 asks you to briefly plan a lesson. The lesson includes two sessions of less than one hour each, spread over two days. Your lesson must meet the standards-based learning goals given in the case study, and it must meet the developmental needs of the students, both individually and as a class. The case study describes a content area unit and a hypothetical class of students, including their needs and interests. It is very important that you explicitly connect what you know about the students and the content in your plan. Review terms used in Case Study 1 before you plan and analyze your lesson.

Your instructional planning and strategies will help you in the next CalTPA task, Designing Instruction (DI), and in the Culminating Teaching Experience. Both require you to plan your own lesson.

CalTPA Terms

SSP Case Study 1

Learning experience	A set of events that help students master specified content; in this case, a rough synonym for *lesson*.
Unit	A series of lessons or learning experiences that addresses the same topic. Units typically last from four to six weeks, but can be shorter or longer.

Learning goals	Intended outcomes for a lesson or unit. Goals specify what students should know or do as a result of the lesson or unit. Some educators use the term objectives (very specific, student-oriented outcomes) for lessons and think of broader goals for units. The CalTPA does not make such a distinction.
Instructional resources	Available materials, including text, objects, supplies, and technology-based tools. Subsequent CalTPA tasks include personnel as instructional resources.
Developmental needs	Needs that are predictable based on typical patterns of human growth. Development includes physical, cognitive, social, and emotional components.
Lesson	A set of events designed to help students master a limited amount of content. Lessons typically have just a few goals and address a single specific topic. Lessons are often about an hour in length, but can be longer or shorter depending on factors like the age of the students.
Instructional strategies	Pedagogical techniques a teacher intentionally employs during instruction. The CalTPA equates instructional strategies with "what the teacher does."
Student activities	Expected student behaviors during instruction. CalTPA equates student activities with "what the student does." Example: As an instructional strategy, a teacher might read aloud. The corresponding student activity is listening to the read-aloud.

As is the case with all CalTPA tasks, you download the template, save it with a special file name, and type directly into the template. For Case Study 1, you type your lesson into the expandable boxes that look like this:

Instructional Strategies	Student Activities

Although this format may be different from the lesson planning format you use during your credential program or in your classroom, it is still a set of steps—a procedure—for what you and the students will do so that students master the learning goals. You may choose the voice, or format, you use in your plan. Running narrative description and bulleted or numbered formats are both common. However, make certain that the steps you and the students would take during the two-day lesson are clear. You are writing *a plan*. Practice identifying, pairing, and sequencing instructional strategies and student activities with the *You Try It! Lesson Sort*.

You Try It!

Lesson Sort

Read the lettered list. Place each one in the correct column, pairing an instructional strategy with a student activity. List them in the proper sequence. The first two are done for you. It might help you to first sort them into "what the teacher does" and "what the student does." Then pair them and sequence them in a logical order. Check your answers in the Appendix.

Fourth-grade physical education learning goal: Students will jump a self-turned rope.

Instructional Strategies	Student Activity
b. Show a fluid model of jumping a self-turned rope.	d. Watch a fluid model of jumping a self-turned rope.

a. Listen to feedback about progress to date. Give a personal goal for jump roping.
~~b. Show a fluid model of jumping a self-turned rope.~~
c. Bring the class together and provide feedback on their progress. Ask for their next jump roping goals.
~~d. Watch a fluid model of jumping a self-turned rope.~~
e. Lead a discussion about what the class notices about the fluid model of jumping rope.
f. Apply the steps for jumping rope by jumping rope.
g. Watch the demonstration of the steps of jumping rope.
h. Demonstrate the steps of jumping rope.
i. Distribute jump ropes to partners and monitor as they apply the steps of jumping rope.
j. Participate in a discussion about the critical attributes of the fluid model of jumping rope.

Some candidates ask how much detail to include in the expandable lesson boxes. Remember that CalTPA scorers are looking for evidence of your knowledge and skills. They cannot give you credit for evidence you do not record. Also, recall the criteria given in the rubrics. A Score Level 4 response includes evidence that *clearly, consistently,* and *convincingly* demonstrates knowledge and skills. Evidence must also be *clear or detailed.* Use these criteria to help you decide how much detail to include; there is no penalty for including too much detail as long as it is *clear, accurate, specific,* and *appropriate.*

Case Study 1 Suggestion: Check for Lesson Component Connections

When you plan a lesson, the instructional strategies, student activities, and resources must be connected and support the specific learning goals. Components also need to be connected to the class's needs and interests.

Ensuring connectedness begins with the content standards. Before planning your Case Study 1 lesson, study the given content standards and highlight key words. Note that the given learning goals may not address each component of the stated standards. Lessons often address just a portion of a standard; earlier or later lessons may address the remaining components. Study the standard, looking for verbs, and circle the behaviors or knowledge that students are expected to exhibit as a result of your lesson—for example, explain, determine, translate, compute. Plan your lesson to ensure that students can do every one of those goals by the end of the lesson. *CalTPA Trouble Shooting Tip: Help Students Hit the Targets!* addresses how to use a standard to plan a lesson.

CalTPA Trouble Shooting Tip

Help Students Hit the Targets!

Plan to provide actual instruction to help students reach the learning goals. For example, if a lesson goal is based on the standard "students will analyze plot structure," your lesson needs to *teach students* how to analyze plot structure. Simply assigning them a plot to analyze is an inadequate response for the CalTPA. If students understood how to analyze plot structure, you would not be teaching this lesson. What could you do to help students analyze plot structure? There are many appropriate instructional choices. You might present components of plot structure, model how to find these components, analyze a plot together, and use partner activities in which students analyze a plot together before analyzing a different one alone. There is a difference between *assigning* a standard and helping students *reach it.*

Make sure that the strategies are appropriate for the lesson goals and student needs. Practice identifying inappropriate strategies and activities in *You Try It! Odd Man Out.*

You Try It!

Odd Man Out

Read the contextual information, then choose which of the three instructional strategies and students activities is least appropriate *for the lesson goal or needs of the class. Explain your reasoning. Check your work against ours in the Appendix.*

Contextual Information

Grade: Seven
Learning goal: Students explain and give examples of how fossils provide evidence of how life and environmental conditions have changed.

Class description: The class is a GATE cluster, with most students identified as gifted or working above grade level in science. Students have little time after school for homework and have limited access to the Internet outside of school. They enjoy working in groups but need help using their class time well.

Developmental needs: Students experience intense peer pressure. They enjoy projects that involve actual materials and link to their own experiences.

Set One: Instructional Strategies:

a. Teacher leads a round-robin reading of the fossil chapter. He listens carefully for clear oral reading fluency and helps students with words they cannot pronounce.

b. Teacher presents a fossil and has students infer facts about the animal's life and the conditions under which it lived.

c. Teacher provides instruction on how to work with a partner and manage time effectively and then gives each pair a fossil, a printout of information about that fossil, and a series of writing prompts that ask students to explain how the fossil provides evidence of life long ago.

Which is the Odd Man Out? Why?

_____

_____

_____

Set Two: Student Activities (Note: These activities don't link to above instructional strategies.)

a. Students handle fossils and search the Internet to find the environmental conditions that created the fossils.

b. Students independently read two pages in the textbook and answer a multiple choice quiz to identify fossils.

c. Students work in cooperative groups to analyze their group's fossil and together write a one-paragraph analysis of the evidence it provides of changing conditions. Every student must put pen to paper in the paragraph.

Which is the Odd Man Out? Why?

_____

_____

_____

You should now feel confident that you can complete Case Study 1. Before moving on to Case Study 2, use this *You Try It! Put Your Finger on It!* self-assessment to check that your instructional components support each other, address student needs, and work toward the learning goals.

		Yes	Not Yet
	You Try It!		
	Put Your Finger on It! Self-Assessing Your Response to Case Study 1		
1.	In the template, put your finger on the lesson goals. Then check your plan to ensure that you have addressed every lesson goal with your instructional strategies and student activities.		
2.	Put your finger on the class description and on developmental needs. (You summarized this information in your *Charting the SSP* table.) Then check your plan to find specific ways that you have incorporated students' needs and interests in your lesson. How many specific examples can you find? Are there better, more appropriate connections you could make?		
3.	Put your finger on the available resources in the template. Then check your plan to see that you made full use of them.		
4.	Put your finger on the given content standards. Then check that your plan works toward those standards (as appropriate for the learning goals).		
5.	Does your plan include pedagogy and instructional strategies that are appropriate for the content area? How?		

GETTING SPECIFIC: CASE STUDY 2

SSP Case Study 2 asks you to analyze an assessment plan. The case study gives you information about a unit of instruction related to your credential area; a hypothetical teacher's plan to assess student learning goals for the instructional experience; and the dissatisfied teacher's reflection on the plan. Your analysis of the assessment plan must describe a strength and weakness. Then the case study presents another assessment for this unit; your response must explain how you would use this assessment and describe the strengths of your usage.

The skills you demonstrate in SSP Case Study 2, Assessment Practices, will be helpful to you in a subsequent CalTPA task, Assessing Learning (AL). In AL, you build on your assessment knowledge, and skills by choosing or developing and implementing your own assessment and then analyzing the experience. The Culminating Teaching Experience also includes assessment.

To earn a Score Level 4 on the SSP, you must demonstrate that you use assessment to guide instruction and choose feedback strategies. You must provide evidence that you have a clear and accurate understanding of the purposes and uses of different types of assessments and that you know multiple measures for assessing students' knowledge, skills and abilities. First, make sure that you understand assessment-related terms and principles used in Case Study 2.

CalTPA Terms

SSP Case Study 2

Assessment Type	The kind or nature of the assessment, such as informal or formal, formative or summative, and format (such as multiple choice, essay, and fill in the blank).
Purpose	The reason for the assessment. One assessment can serve different purposes depending on how it is used. Also, an assessment can be highly effective for one purpose and ineffective for others. Teachers must be mindful of their purposes as they select their assessments.
Implementation	The conditions under which an assessment is used. This includes factors such as how many students work together on the assessment (individual, partner, small group), the time allotted, who corrects the assessment, and the resources students are allowed to use during the assessment.
Feedback Strategies	The techniques employed to give students (and others) information about student performance on the assessment. Feedback strategies also include the types of information shared regarding student performance.
Diagnostic	An assessment that provides information about entry-level (pre-instructional) performance (knowledge, skills, or abilities). Some educators consider diagnostic assessments as a subset of formative assessments.
Formative Assessment	Assessment that is used, in immediate ways, to shape instruction. Occurs during instruction.
Summative Assessment	Assessment that is used to provide a post-instructional—or summary—measure of student performance. Occurs at the end of a significant instructional sequence such as a chapter, unit, semester, or year.
Informal Assessment	Assessment that provides information about student performance in ways that are less than systematic. It provides the teacher with a higher degree of uncertainty about what each individual student knows and can do. Informal assessment information may be gathered without recording data for each student (e.g., students quickly flash thumbs up or down) or from assignments completed outside of class (e.g., students work on a book report at home).
Formal Assessment	Assessment that collects information in a systematic way. Formal assessments typically provide information about each student under carefully specified conditions. Results often factor into student grades. Examples include written individual tests taken during class.
Misconceptions	Ideas that students hold about the content that are contrary to accepted concepts or ways of thinking. Misconceptions (or alternative conceptions) are deeper than factual knowledge and are a natural part of human learning. Assessments need to tap into students' deeply held notions rather than solely skimming the surface of their factual knowledge.
Multiple Measures	The many forms of assessment used to provide a valid (accurate) and reliable (consistent) picture of student performance. Teachers must use a variety of measures to adequately measure student performance.

Case Study 2 Suggestion: Check for Assessment Plan Connections

As is the case for Case Study 1's lesson components, Case Study 2's assessment plan components must also be tightly connected. First, the assessments must be driven by the learning goals. For each learning goal in the assessment plan, check that it is appropriately measured by one or more assessments. Try *You Try It! Looking for Links* to practice matching assessment to learning goals.

You Try It!

Looking for Links

Circle the three examples where the assessment most clearly matches the K–12 standards-based learning goal. Check your work against ours in the Appendix.

Learning Goal	Assessment Type
1. Students will perform character-based monologues, using voice, blocking, and gesture.	Essay test scored with a rubric
2. Students will safely use hand and power tools, machines, and equipment.	Observation with checklist
3. Students will count by 2s, 5s, and 10s to 100.	Oral test (coins allowed as manipulatives)
4. Students will use simple and compound sentences in speaking.	Multiple choice quiz
5. Spanish 2 students will correctly conjugate regular verbs in the preterite tense (one form of past tense).	Vocabulary test (Students write the vocabulary terms they hear while listening to a recording of a native Spanish speaker.)
6. Chemistry students will use Le Chatelier's principle to predict the effect of changes in concentration, temperature, and pressure.	Short-answer test with realistic problems related to changes in concentration, temperature, and pressure.

As you check that standards-based learning goals are clearly linked to assessments, also ask if the given assessments are the most appropriate ways to check student performance related to the goal. For example, do any of the assessments have the potential to identify student misconceptions? There may be assessments that are a more efficient or more productive means to check student progress.

Your assessment plan should also measure students' growth over time. Effective teachers use assessment before, during, and after instruction in order to gain accurate information about student learning, and they use the information they have gathered over time to shape instruction. Check that assessment components include:

- Entry-level information that helps the teacher plan instruction
- Formative assessment that helps the teacher adjust lessons during instruction
- Summative assessment that provides a "final" view of how well students have mastered content

Assessments at each stage are not just helpful to the teacher; they should also help students set their own goals and monitor their own progress.

For assessment information to be useful to students, students must receive feedback on their performance. Check that assessment components use appropriate feedback strategies for students to learn about their own performance. As appropriate, feedback strategies should also provide information to others, such as family members. Here are some examples of feedback strategies:

- Having students grade their own work and review their performance
- Giving students their corrected work and discussing results
- Holding writing or portfolio conferences with students
- Using dialogue journals about student learning
- Utilizing peer grading according to a rubric
- Requiring students to analyze their errors after exams
- Employing authors' circles in which students respond to each other's work according to specified criteria
- Sharing or having students create and analyze photographs or line graphs that indicate change in their performance over time
- Sending performance-based notes home to families
- Sharing information with families via phone calls, informal conversations, newsletters, blogs, or websites
- Holding parent conferences

Teachers should have a clear plan for how they will use assessment information to adjust their instruction. As a general rule, teachers should collect classroom assessment data only if they can use the results. For instance, if a large number of students receive "below basic" scores on an assessment, the teacher is obliged to analyze the types of errors students are making and provide instructional interventions to bring students to proficient or advanced levels of performance. Check the assessment plan to ensure that the assessment data can be used to improve future instruction and learning related to content goals.

An assessment plan should connect the various assessments. Teachers use multiple measures to gain an accurate picture of student learning. Check that the specified assessments work in concert to provide a holistic portrait of student performance related to content goals. Understanding the many assessments available to you can help you use multiple measures effectively. Use *You Try It! Sort It Out!* for practice here.

You Try It!

Sort It Out!

Write the letter of each assessment in the boxes where it belongs. Write each letter twice: once in a Timing *box and once in a* Formality *box. There may be many places where a single assessment fits. For simplicity, go with your judgment of the* most common *use of the assessment. One is done for you. Compare your answers with ours in the Appendix.*

Timing	Diagnostic	
	Formative	
	Summative	a. Standardized tests
Formality	Informal	
	Formal	a. Standardized tests

a. Standardized tests
b. White boards (students write on them and hold them up during a lesson)
c. Chapter quizzes
d. Essays
e. Reflective journals
f. Multimedia presentations (e.g., PowerPoint, podcasts)
g. Quick writes or sketches
h. Unison response (the class shouts out an answer together at the teacher's signal)
i. Informal Reading Inventory

As a final tip for Case Study 2, remember to use specific professional terminology that demonstrates your accurate, clear, specific, and detailed understanding of assessment practices. Check your response by highlighting assessment-related terminology; consider how you would defend your choices; and look for even more appropriate choices for assessing student learning in relation to learning goals.

GETTING SPECIFIC: CASE STUDY 3

Case Study 3 asks you to adapt instruction for the needs of a hypothetical English learner. The case study gives you a description of a standards-based unit with details about two days of instruction; information about the English learner, including background, academic attainment, and home language (Spanish); and the student's CELDT level and language samples. Your task is to analyze the student's learning needs, identify challenges the given instruction will present for her or him, suggest and defend some instructional adaptations, consider how you might monitor the student's progress, and think about next steps for facilitating English language development.

Your response to Case Study 3 must demonstrate your knowledge of subject-specific, developmentally appropriate instruction that meets two goals for your English learner: content development and English language development.

The skills you demonstrate in SSP Case Study 3, Adaptation of Subject-Specific Pedagogy for English Learners, will be helpful to you in the CalTPA tasks Designing Instruction, Assessing Learning, and Culminating Teaching Experience. These tasks all require you to adapt instruction for an actual English learner.

The table contains terms you should know when you complete Case Study 3.

CalTPA Terms	
SSP Case Study 3	
Progress Monitoring	Formative assessment. Assists teachers in determining students' performance during instruction so that the teacher can modify instruction in response to students' current attainment and needs.
CELDT	California English Language Development Test. A test required for all California K–12 students whose primary language is not English. The CELDT identifies levels of English development in listening and speaking, reading, and writing. Review Chapter 5 for detailed information about CELDT. Visit the CELDT page of the Department of Education's website at http://celdt.cde.ca.gov/.
English Language Development	English acquisition. Focuses on students' progress to attain fluency in the English language. One of the two major goals for English learners. See the English Language Development Standards at the Department of Education's website (http://www.cde.ca.gov/be/st/ss/documents/englangdevstnd.pdf) for standards that help English learners develop proficiency in English.

Specially Designed Content Instruction	Not specifically a term in the CalTPA, specially designed content instruction (sometimes called specially designed academic instruction in English, or SDAIE) focuses on the second of two goals for English learners: mastery of grade-level, standards-based content despite partial fluency in English. Review Chapter 5 for suggestions on designing content instruction in English for English learners.

Case Study 3 Suggestion: Link Student Needs, Learning Goals, and the Road to Get There

Case Study 3 asks you to answer five prompts, along with a few sub-prompts. You must understand the English learner's needs and then adjust instruction so that the student can do two things: (1) meet content-based learning goals and (2) develop English language skills. As is the case with all CalTPA tasks, standards-based content learning goals drive it all. Your job is to analyze student needs and use your expertise to link those content goals and student needs. In Case Study 3, it is essential that you analyze the path (instruction) that leads the student to the goals. Use the following steps to link learning goals, student needs, and instruction:

1. Analyze the standards-based learning goals to be clear about what students need to learn. For a concise summary, check your work on *Charting the SSP*.
2. Read the student's oral and written language samples, looking for patterns that support classification of the student's English development level.
3. Review the knowledge and skills that describe the student's level of English acquisition. (You can review *Chapter 5: Making Adaptations for English Learners* or the English Language Development standards and materials found at the Department of Education's website, http://www.celdt.org/).
4. Review the knowledge and skills possessed by students who are one level above your given student in their language acquisition. Consider the actual steps you would need to take to bring your student from the current level of English development to the next.
5. Review the five general principles for facilitating English language development and content mastery (found in Chapter 5) and identify the ways in which the instruction in Case Study 3 violates those principles. Also consult the professional materials you've amassed during your credential program.
6. Think of alternatives that embody—rather than violate—those principles.
7. Justify how your alternatives will help the student meet the two goals of content mastery and English language and will help you monitor the student's progress.

For practice in adapting practices for English language development and content mastery, use *You Try It! There's Gotta Be a Better Way!*

You Try It!

There's Gotta Be a Better Way!

For each traditional instructional scenario in the left column, create two or more appropriate EL adaptations for a student whose CELDT score places her at the Intermediate level. Chapter 5: Making Adaptations for English Learners contains good suggestions. Justify how your adaptations support the goals of both English language development and content mastery for your English learner. Compare your work with ours in the Appendix.

1. The teacher presents a textbook-driven lecture on fifteen major points. Students take notes, then pack up when the bell rings and leave.	
2. To synthesize what they have learned, the students write 45-minute independent in-class essays on causes of the Great Depression.	
3. During a whole-class discussion, students who raise their hands contribute individual definitions with supporting details on their concept of loneliness.	
4. Before the lesson, the teacher presents a list of ten vocabulary terms and students work in pairs to look up and record definitions in their individual journals.	

Review your Case Study 3 response to ensure that it meets the criteria for a Score Level 4 response. Ask yourself whether you have provided *clear, specific, accurate, and detailed* evidence. Also check that you not only provide content-specific, developmentally appropriate instruction for standards-based learning goals. Do your teaching strategies and instruction promote English language development?

GETTING SPECIFIC: CASE STUDY 4

Case Study 4 is similar to Case Study 3 in that it presents an instructional experience and asks you to adapt it for the needs of a hypothetical student. This time, however, the student is a native English speaker and has a set of special needs—a learning disability plus others. The case study gives you a description of a standards-based unit with details about a few days of instruction. Case Study 4, like Case Study 3, presents information about the student's educational history and current needs. And, just as for Case Study 3, your task is to identify challenges the given instruction will present for the student, suggest and defend instructional adaptations, and consider how you might monitor the student's progress. Specifically, the three prompts (and sub-prompts) for Case Study 4 require you to:

- Analyze and adapt instruction for the student's *learning disability* and then justify your adaptation
- Analyze and adapt instruction for *an additional need* of the student and then justify your adaptation
- Analyze and adapt *progress monitoring assessment* based on student needs

The skills you demonstrate in Case Study 4 will be helpful to you in CalTPA tasks Designing Instruction, Assessing Learning, and Culminating Teaching Experience, which all require you to adapt instruction for an actual learner with special needs.

Before you begin, look back at *Try It! Charting the SSP* and double-check that our summary of Case Study 4 matches your interpretation. Review important terms used in Case Study 4. Some of these terms may not appear in your version of the SSP.

CalTPA Terms	
SSP Case Study 4	
Asthma	An inflammatory disorder of the airways (respiratory system) that makes breathing difficult during an attack. Can vary from intermediate to severe (with some severe cases leading to death). Treated through medication and by avoiding conditions (e.g., dust, exertion, pollen) that trigger attacks.
Attention Deficit Hyperactivity Disorder (ADHD)	A disorder, believed to be neurological, that results in individuals having problems in the following areas: impulsivity, hyperactivity, boredom, and inattention. Individuals can display either inattentive disorder (ADD), hyperactivity disorder (HD), or both. Often occurs with other specific learning disabilities.
General Education	Standard, unmodified classroom setting and curriculum. Services all students without identified special needs and, for some portion of the day, many students with identified special needs as well. Formerly called "regular education."

Individualized Education Program (IEP)	A plan for education that is specific and appropriate to address a student's individual needs. Required by federal law for students with identified special educational needs. Identifies annual goals, steps to meet the goals, and team responsibilities.
Resource Specialist Program (RSP)	Also called "Resource." A form of special education that services students with identified special needs for a portion of the school day. Students spend some portion of each day in their general education classroom and some in the Resource setting. Alternatively, a Resource Specialist may work with students with identified needs while in the general education classroom. Most students with Specific Learning Disabilities are served through the Resource Specialist Program.
Special Education	Range of services provided to students with special needs based upon students' individual, identified needs. Review Chapter 6 for laws regarding special education services.
Specific Learning Disability	A disorder in the psychological process(es) for understanding or applying language. Results in imperfect abilities to listen, think, speak, read, write, spell, or calculate. Does not include disorders related to physical conditions, such as vision or hearing loss, or those related to disadvantages related to environment, culture, or economics. (See Section 300.8 of the Individuals with Disabilities Education Act [2004], http://idea.ed.gov/explore/view/p/,root,regs,300,A,300%252E8. Most students identified as having specific learning disabilities have disabilities related to reading [http://nces.ed.gov/fastfacts/display.asp?id=64]).

Case Study 4 Suggestion: Do Whatever It Takes (DWIT)

Chapter 6: Making Adaptations for Learners with Special Needs began with these words: "Every student *can* learn. Every student *has a right* to learn. It's your responsibility to ensure that every student *does* learn." Indeed, for a Score Level 4, the SSP rubric requires you to adapt a lesson for the student with special needs *based on information about the student*. Your response needs to provide *connected, accurate, appropriate, relevant,* and *clear* or *detailed* evidence to show that you know how to meet those needs.

The following five suggestions for your Case Study 4 response should help you demonstrate your competence in adapting instruction and assessment so that all students can master content-based goals and further their development as individuals.

1. *Study special needs.* How much do you really know about asthma? One author (Andrea) met the following student health needs during one year as a middle school teacher: osteogenesis imperfecta, adolescent-onset diabetes, seizure disorder, and hemophilia. Use your peers, other professionals, text resources, and the Internet to learn about these issues. Chapter 6 provided many web addresses that will increase your knowledge in adapting instruction for students with special needs. *DWIT to learn about your students' needs.*

2. *Remember that you are teaching people.* Development is cognitive, social, physical, and emotional. Think about your SSP student with special needs the way you think about all of your students: holistically, and as a person who has many developing facets. *DWIT to help your student grow in every area.*

3. *Think about short-term and long-term solutions.* Given the many demands of the general education classroom, it's often tempting to go with the course of action that helps events flow smoothly. For example, a teacher might not hold a student who has an explosive temper to the same rules of conduct as other students. Avoiding conflict certainly provides a comfortable *short-term solution.* However, it robs the student of the *long-term* opportunity to learn strategies for managing situations she finds emotionally difficult. Don't just make life easier for your students today; gently, kindly, and consistently teach them the skills that will allow them to make their own lives easier tomorrow. *DWIT to help students gain skills for life.*

4. *Consider accommodations and modifications.* Chapter 6 distinguishes between the two. Unless the student has an educational plan or has presented clear evidence that he needs modified content goals, expect him to meet the same standards as other students. *Accommodate* your instructional strategies to provide him every opportunity to meet grade-level standards. As a side note for subsequent CalTPA tasks, students who are working above grade level or are gifted usually need you to shift your expectations upward. *DWIT to keep expectations high.*

5. *Adapt assessments.* Students deserve every opportunity to demonstrate what they learn. If your selected assessments block students from demonstrating their progress, then the assessments will provide an inaccurate view of student learning. Look at the student's specific learning needs and ensure that your selected assessment does not create barriers between the student and demonstration of learning. As an example, a fifth-grade student with a spelling disability may be able to recite and locate on a map all U.S. states and their capitals but will struggle with spelling words like Cheyenne, Tallahassee, Des Moines, and Baton Rouge. Has the student mastered the fifth-grade standard of knowing states and capitals? *DWIT to allow students to show what they know.*

Practice putting these suggestions into place with *You Try It! DWIT ... or Not.*

You Try It!

DWIT . . . or Not

Each scenario violates one or even more of the suggestions for Doing Whatever It Takes to adapt instruction and assessment for special needs. However, match each scenario with just one suggestion. Use each number once. Compare your response to the key in the Appendix.

1. DWIT to learn about your students' needs.
2. DWIT to help your student grow in every area.
3. DWIT to help students gain skills for life.
4. DWIT to keep expectations high.
5. DWIT to allow students to show what they know.

Scenario	DWIT suggestion violated
a. Your student has an IEP for speech. You allow him to skip the oral report that serves as an assessment for the current topic. Instead you record a B for the assessment next to the student's name in your grade spreadsheet.	
b. You have a six-year-old first-grader who is highly gifted (I.Q of 200). He has no friends in your class. He feels that his peers pick on him, and they feel that he is a show off. To adapt to his giftedness, you allow him to work alone at his own level or to spend afternoons in the fourth-grade class two doors down.	
c. You have a student with achondroplasia (a prevalent form of dwarfism). So as not to embarrass him during your basketball unit, you send him to the library during physical education.	
d. You have a student on the autism spectrum. You adapt instruction to keep her stimulated. You encourage lots of different settings, personnel, and routines to keep the student stimulated.	
e. You have a student who has a clear and documented history of struggling to organize her materials. To help her, you give her an F for every day that she comes to class with her notebook out of order.	

As you complete Case Study 4, you may find it easier to complete because of your familiarity with the format of the tasks and with the content they assess.

Chapter Summary

Each of the four case studies in Subject Specific Pedagogy provides an opportunity for you to demonstrate your ability to bring together student needs and content goals in order to effect powerful standards-based learning for all your students. Every teacher is a learner. What would you like to learn next related to content from the Subject Specific Pedagogy task? To celebrate completion of your first CalTPA task, consider the *Ponder This*.

PONDER THIS...

Teachers are learners. Subject Specific Pedagogy measures your competence in bringing content standards and kids together—at an initial level. You will continue to increase your knowledge and skills in meeting students' needs over the course of your career. For your future reference, list three subject-specific pedagogy questions or topics (*English language development? developmental appropriateness? specific learning disabilities?*) that you want to learn more about.

8

■ ■ ■

Designing Instruction

*"Get to know your students from
the beginning and the rest is a breeze."*
—RUTH REINKER, SUCCESSFUL CALTPA
DESIGNING INSTRUCTION CANDIDATE

At the heart of effective instruction is a sound lesson plan that is based on the needs of the students. It is vitally important that teachers plan lessons based on what they know about their students and connect their knowledge of students with the learning goals. Designing Instruction will help you demonstrate your ability to plan a developmentally appropriate, standards-based lesson that incorporates your knowledge of students. This chapter presents support in the following sections:

- Overview of the Designing Instruction Task
- What Is Being Assessed in the Designing Instruction Task?
- Comparing Designing Instruction and Subject Specific Pedagogy
- Step 1: Subject Matter, Learning Goals, Information About Students
- Step 2: Learning About Two Focus Students
- Step 3: Planning for Whole Class Instruction
- Step 4: Making Adaptations for Two Focus Students
- Step 5: Reflecting

OVERVIEW OF THE DESIGNING INSTRUCTION TASK

The Designing Instruction (DI) task gives you the opportunity to demonstrate your ability to plan a lesson based on California state content standards and student characteristics. You must fulfill these requirements:

- Identify subject area and learning goals.
- Identify what you would like to know about students and what methods you could use to find this information.
- Learn about the characteristics of two chosen focus students (an English learner and a student with a different instructional challenge).
- Plan instruction that addresses those student characteristics.
- Reflect on your ability to connect learning about students to instructional planning.

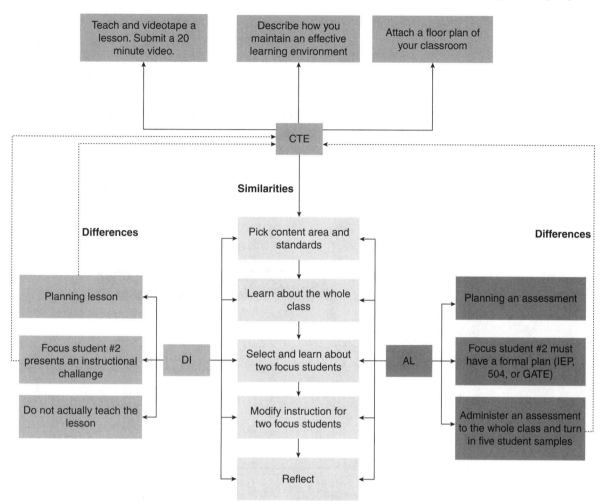

Comparisons of CalTPA Tasks: Designing Instruction, Assessing Learning, and Culminating Teaching Experience

all students. A few examples of active teaching techniques include the following:

1. Individual wipe boards: Provide each student with a wipe board and a dry erase marker. Pose a question and give students time to respond. Ask students to hold up their responses.

2. Think-pair-share: Ask a question, then provide "think time." Have partners discuss their thinking and share with the class.

3. Give One, Get One: Pose a question and ask students to write their responses on paper. Ask students to circulate around the room and share and listen to responses of atleast three different students.

4. Four corners: Pose a question with four different options. Label each corner of the room as one of the answer choices. Ask students to go to the corner that matches their responses.

5. Carousel: Place photos, artwork, artifacts, or other materials in different areas around the outer perimeter of the classroom. Ask students to form small groups. Have each small group circulate to view, discuss, and analyze the materials.

Consider your role in the classroom. How can you encourage students to use higher-level thinking skills, exploration, and inquiry? Put yourself in your students' place. Would you be interested by your lesson introduction? If you think you might be bored and disconnected from the content, then chances are your students will feel the same way.

Follow the hook with a logical lesson body. The delivery of the content depends on the teaching approach you select. You can either use inductive or deductive teaching strategies. Regardless of the approach, it is critical that you use sound pedagogical strategies to deliver the content. For example, if you are teaching a lesson that includes reading, do not randomly call on students to read aloud selected text. Although many teachers think this strategy, called popcorn reading, is appropriate for decoding and fluency practice, it promotes anxiety for those students who struggle with fluency, and it decreases comprehension for other students if the delivery is choppy or inaccurate (Pennington, 2009). Use *You Try It! Pass on the Popcorn* to think of alternatives.

You Try It!

Pass on the Popcorn

How many appropriate and effective reading strategies can you think of to replace popcorn reading? Record them below. Compare your ideas with ours in the Appendix.

Finally, after teaching your objectives through your lesson body, end your lesson and emphasize the key points presented in the lesson body during your close. Again, ensure active participation by all students. Independent practice is a good way to complete a lesson.

How will you determine individual student progress? How can you determine whether or not each student mastered the lesson objectives? CTE requires you to analyze student learning and to submit five student samples to support your analysis. Think about how you will assess student learning throughout your lesson. Even though you use informal assessment strategies during the body of the lesson to check for understanding and make mid-lesson adjustments to your teaching plan, it would not be wise to submit informal assessment data collected during instruction; it might be difficult to track and report five individual responses on a checklist or collect anecdotal records while you are also teaching and monitoring the progress of the entire class. Instead, think about how you can assess individual student learning after instruction and use those individual samples to support your analysis of student learning.

Instructional Approaches

Instructional models or approaches include direct instruction, learning cycle, guided and unguided inquiry, concept formation, and concept attainment. During CalTPA you are not evaluated on the instructional approach you select; however, it makes sense to choose an instructional approach to organize and build your lesson. A brief recap of the steps included in one version of the direct instruction and learning cycle models follows. Remember, there are different versions of each model.

Direct Instruction (Guillaume, 2008, p.144)

1. Open: Anticipatory Set
   - Focus
   - Objective
   - Purpose
2. Body:
   - Teacher Input: Provide clear information related to the objective. One or more of the following may be appropriate: present definitions, share critical attributes, give examples and nonexamples, model.
   - Check for understanding
3. Guided Practice: Students practice the objective as the teacher circulates to provide feedback.
4. Close: Students perform an objective without assistance.
5. Independent Practice: Students practice on their own without teacher feedback.

Learning Cycle

An alternative to direct instruction, the learning cycle is an inductive approach to instruction. It's a cycle because it begins and ends in the real world. One popular version of the learning cycle employs the following four stages (Guillaume, 2008, p.154):

1. Open: Engage students to think about a real world phenomenon, problem, or issue. Raise students' questions.
2. Body:
   - Explore: Students explore phenomenon through direct experience. Exploration is guided by student questions.
   - Develop: Ideas and concepts are developed through reading and discussions.
3. Close: Students apply learning by addressing a new problem or situation.

Regardless of the instructional model you choose for your CTE lesson, your lesson should employ effective practices. Consider your instructional skills using *You Try It! How Not to Teach.*

You Try It!

How Not to Teach

Read the following scenario and identify what is wrong with this teacher's lesson. What instructional strategies is he using? Make recommendations that might improve this lesson. Compare your ideas with ours in the Appendix.

The bell rings. Thirty-five high school juniors shuffle into Mr. John's classroom for their U.S. history class. Mr. John is standing at the front of the room with his history textbook. After the students get settled, Mr. John asks students to get out their textbook and turn to page 37. All 35 students groan. He ignores the groans and explains that today the class is going to talk about slavery in the United States. He calls on Susie to read the first paragraph. After Susie finishes reading, Mr. John summarizes the content and asks if anyone has any questions. He continues with his lesson and calls on Jorge to read the next paragraph. After Jorge finishes reading, Mr. John asks a few questions. The same three students raise their hands and are called upon during this portion of the lesson. The other 32 students stare at their textbooks or off into space to avoid eye contact with the teacher. This same scenario—read and asks questions—continues for the next 20 minutes. At the end of the lesson, Mr. John assigns the 20 vocabulary words at the end of the chapter along with the 10 questions in the chapter review. The students are given 15 minutes in class to work on the assignment and are told to complete the rest for homework. The bell rings. The students come to life and begin eagerly chatting with their friends as they file out of the classroom.

CTE STEP 1: LEARNING ABOUT STUDENTS IN THE WHOLE CLASS AND TWO FOCUS STUDENTS

The CTE *Learning About Students* section has three parts. In Part A, follow the directions to record the class demographics on the class profile sheet. Parts B and C require you to learn about the whole class and your two focus students. Your two focus students for this task include an English learner and another student who presents a different instructional challenge. Focus student two does not need to have a formal plan on file to document the instructional challenge. Perhaps the student is gifted or shy or has a health need or has trouble engaging with instruction. Any of these issues require you to think a bit harder about how to reach the student and build success. Review *CalTPA Tip: Keep It Real* to help you select focus students. Remember, CalTPA requires different focus students for each task. You can not use the same focus students who were used in previous tasks. There are many different strategies you can use to learn about your students. Checking cumulative files, administering surveys,

CalTPA Tip

Keep It Real

Presenting random student data without clear connections or relevance to the lesson is one of the most common mistakes candidates make in the Learning About Students section of the CTE. For example, if you include the detail that your English learner wants to be a police officer, find a way to connect this information to the content area selected for your CalTPA task. If your content area is social studies, this detail would be relevant because it connects to community, local government, citizenship, and geography. Be sure that you explicitly show the relevance of the data you collect and analyze.

and conducting interviews are a few examples. Refer back to the CalTPA tip shared in Chapter 8: *Gather information about students from a variety of sources* for more ideas.

CTE STEP 2: LEARNING ENVIRONMENT AND ACADEMIC INSTRUCTIONAL PLANNING FOR THE WHOLE CLASS

In Step 2 you are asked "In what ways do you establish and maintain a positive climate for learning?" Your response should include a detailed lesson plan in which you identify best practices for establishing and maintaining an effective learning environment.

Learning Environment

If the teacher cannot effectively manage the classroom, then even the best lesson plan on paper can result in a disaster. The first step for establishing a positive learning environment involves building healthy relationships among students and with the teacher. All individuals should be respected, valued, and have a voice in the learning community. A few ideas for building and supporting a classroom community follow. Some refer to one-time activities and others are ongoing.

1. Classroom Meetings: Take time each day or week to discuss issues or concerns affecting the students in your classroom. The concerns discussed at the classroom meeting are generally presented by the students. Issues might relate to arguments on the playground, the noise level in the lunchroom, the classroom arrangement, or community or global issues.

2. Classroom Puzzle: Draw a jigsaw puzzle on a piece of poster board and cut it into individual pieces. Make sure every student has a puzzle piece. Encourage students to decorate the puzzle piece to represent themselves. Have students find two other pieces that match their piece and share. Work together as a team to create a class masterpiece.

3. Towers: Provide each team with the same materials. Explain that the task is to build the tallest tower in ten minutes. Encourage students to be creative. Do not give feedback that validates or discourages their ideas. After ten minutes ask students to circulate around the room to observe the strategies used by other teams. Discuss their observations and strategies. Finally, measure the towers to see who built the highest towers.

4. Role-play: Use role-playing scenarios to help students practice conflict resolution.

5. Class Government and Economy: Have students propose the rules, regulate behavior, and monitor expectations using a mock economy system.

Some psychologists have suggested that certain needs must be met before true motivation and learning can occur. For example, William Glasser, a psychiatrist who specialized in choice theory, proposed the idea that our choices are driven by five basic needs: freedom, power, fun, safety, and love. In order to meet these needs, people strive to create relationships with one another that promote trust, acceptance, listening, support, encouragement, compromise, and respect (Glasser, 1986). As a result of his work, many educators strive to create a safe learning environment for all students built around these five basic needs. Regardless of your personal philosophy, one thing is certain: respect is earned, not forced. If you want respect from your students, then you must be willing to give it.

Management Plan

To develop a classroom management system, you must have a clear plan in place that is consistently reinforced. You must be firm, fair, and consistent. How are you going to manage student behavior? If a student chooses to make a poor decision, how will you handle it? What are the consequences? What are the consequences for repeat offenders? How do you help students learn to govern their own behavior? How do you involve students and parents in the process?

Procedures

Identify specific procedures to help accomplish classroom tasks effectively and efficiently. Here are some procedures to consider. Select those that are appropriate for your students' grade level.

- *Beginning the school day or homeroom:* Set routines to: check in on the attendance board; select lunch choice by placing a marble in the appropriate container (choice A, lunchroom, choice B, brought lunch); turn in paperwork in the correct tray (examples include homework, notes from parents, and permission forms); and complete morning work written on the board each morning.
- *Arrive on time:* Give every student two tardy card passes at the beginning of each grading period. If students are tardy, they must turn in one of their cards. After the two tardy passes are used, then a tardy plan with consequences should be in place. If students go the entire grading period without one tardy, they can turn in their tardy cards and receive a reward or incentive of their choice (such as homework pass, free time, lunch with the teacher, extra credit point on an assignment).
- *Ending the school day or class period:* Students should check mailbox, copy homework into planner, pack bag.
- *Leaving the room as a class:* Students can line up by rows, month of birthday, or table groups.
- *Leaving the room independently:* Have students put their clip on a hall pass board when they take a hall pass so that you know who is out of the room in case of an emergency.
- *Bathroom:* Allow one person at a time to go, but preferably not during direct instruction or an activity unless it is an emergency.
- *Distributing and Collecting Materials:* Teacher assistants pass out and collect papers. Collected papers go into boxes in prominent locations.
- *Interruptions or delays:* If you have to stop instruction to talk with a visitor, provide students with some choices while you are otherwise

engaged, such as completing a sponge activity, reading, drawing, relaxing, or finishing an assignment.

- *Housekeeping and student helpers:* Use students for classroom jobs based on their interests. Jobs rotate periodically to ensure equity.
- *Pencil sharpener:* Have two students sharpen several pencils at the end of the day. Students can place their dull pencils in a marked cup next to the sharpener and take a sharpened one from the other cup when necessary.
- *Gaining students' attention:* Use wind chimes, a squeaker toy, rhythm clap, music, verbal cues, or hand signals to focus attention.
- *Student engagement during instruction:* Allow students to toss a ball, stand in a corner to express an opinion, or whip around and share ideas.
- *Student participation:* Pull sticks or cards with student names to ensure equitable and active participation.
- *Cooperative groups:* Pass out a bag of shapes. Each shape represents a different job in the group. After all students select a shape, reveal which job goes with which shape.
- *Turning in assignments:* Attach a magnet to each student's desk. When students complete an assignment they can place it under the magnet for collection. If you teach more than one group of students, designate an assignment tray or file for each period. This will help you separate the paperwork for each class.
- *Noise control:* Teach students the difference between whispering, talking, and silence. Use a traffic light or noise meter to help students monitor volume.
- *Help needed:* To show they need help, students can take a number or place a red cube on their desk. Tell students to "ask three before you ask me." List other strategies on an "I Need Help Chart."
- *Free time:* Choice is critical when students have finished work before the class ends. Provide options such as an extension menu, computer time, reading center, art projects, animal observatory, study hall, writing their own challenge problems, or adding quotations to the class's graffiti board.

Family Communication

Parents and family members are part of the instructional team; keeping parents informed with regular communications about expectations, classroom news, and developments can help parents feel like a part of the team. Ask for their input and always choose your words wisely. Never forget that every student in your classroom is someone's child. Phone calls, newsletters, volunteer opportunities, conferences, emails, and dialogue journals are a few ways to keep parents apprised.

Academic Instruction

The state-adopted academic content standards must directly connect to the learning goals and objectives of your lesson plan. The activities you select for your lesson plan should help students master the academic learning goals. Do not be confused by the CalTPA language. The objective must match the standard. Although the state standards are broad, the academic learning goals are specific and need to be written with language that is measurable and observable. Ask yourself these questions when writing your academic learning goal(s) and plan for instruction: How do you know if students mastered the state-adopted content goals? What activities are you planning to use in your lesson to ensure that students master the academic learning goals and content standards? We addressed aspects of lesson planning in *Chapter 7: Subject Specific Pedagogy, Chapter 8: Designing Instruction,* and in an earlier section of this chapter; be sure you refer back to this information when planning your lesson for CTE. Follow the advice in *CalTPA Tip: CTE Step 2 Part B #10: Don't Be Fooled!*

CalTPA Tip

CTE Step 2 Part B #10: Don't Be Fooled!

In the expandable box for the instructional plan, include all the necessary components of a lesson plan: Open/Body/Close. You also need to address the specific components listed in bold (communicating academic learning goal(s) to students, instructional strategies, student activities, student grouping, materials, and monitoring student learning). You decide how to organize your writing, but consider using headings and formatting options such as bold, italics, and underline to draw attention to each required section of your lesson plan. This helps the assessor to easily identify key components.

CTE STEP 3: LESSON ADAPTATIONS FOR TWO FOCUS STUDENTS

You probably feel like you have demonstrated your ability to make adaptations for English learners and students with other needs in previous tasks. At this stage, you should be able to make adaptations and instructional choices that reflect your level of experience. After all, this is a *culminating* teaching experience. The adaptations you make in this lesson should represent deeper knowledge and skills than you displayed in SSP and DI. What have you learned since then? Before writing this section, review *Chapter 5: Making Adaptations for English Learners* and *Chapter 6: Making Adaptations for Learners with Special Needs* to draw from your strengths on the previous three tasks.

The process of making adaptations begins in CTE Step 1 when you are asked to learn about the students, is supported in Step 2 when you actually use the information about the students to plan the lesson, is made explicit in Step 3 when you make meaningful adaptations to the lesson, is analyzed in Step 5 when you are required to determine whether your lesson and adaptations described in Step 3 were effective, and reflected upon in Step 6 when you are required to explain what you learned about the need for making adaptations. Making direct connections and references to all of the information provided in each step will help to ensure that your response is clear, detailed, and purposefully connected.

CTE STEP 4: TEACHING AND VIDEO RECORDING THE LESSON

In CTE Step 4, you actually teach and videotape your lesson. Before you begin recording, read the information provided here to ensure a high-quality video and compliance with all legal and ethical obligations.

1. Get signed permission from any individual who will appear on camera *before* making the video. You must have signed permission from the parent/guardian of any K–12 student who will appear on the video, as well as any parents, teachers, instructional aides, and other adults. Your teacher preparation program will provide you with information and permission forms to help you comply with these requirements.

2. You may *not* share the video with anyone other than your teacher preparation program.

3. You may *not* use the video for any purpose except the CalTPA CTE task. Do not include the video in your teaching portfolio, use it during an interview, or post it on sites like YouTube or Facebook.

4. The actual video for CTE should be twenty minutes in length; no more, no less. This does not mean that your *lesson* cannot be longer than twenty minutes. However, make sure you showcase your skills on paper and in practice throughout the entire lesson.

5. The video should be unedited. Unfortunately, highlight reels are not accepted. Submit a twenty-minute consecutive segment of video footage that includes best teaching practices. Stay away from footage that includes you lecturing to students at the front of the room or students working silently at their desks for twenty minutes.

6. The video should demonstrate your ability to implement the written lesson plan and manage the classroom. Panning the camera to see student activity and student engagement is important to demonstrate the effectiveness of the lesson.

7. If you have a tripod available, you should use it to prevent shaking and bouncing.

8. Make sure you are using equipment that produces a video with a clear picture and sound.

Make sure you have all your forms, described in *CalTPA Tip: Cross Your T's and Dot Your I's.*

CalTPA Tip

Cross Your T's and Dot Your I's

Be sure you have the appropriate release forms signed for everyone who appears on camera, including adults. You should have the release forms on file before you actually record the lesson. If you are unable to obtain release forms for certain students, they can still participate in the lesson but must be seated out of the camera's range. If this is not possible, remove these students from the classroom to ensure that you do not accidentally include them on the video.

Before you move on to the last two sections of this task, add a clear and concise written description of your teaching context. This is your opportunity to set the stage for what the assessors will be watching. You do not need to give them a play-by-play description of what is going to happen in your lesson; rather, you want to describe any relevant information that might influence your teaching or students' learning. You might want to consider factors such as the physical environment (the arrangement of the desks, temperature, time of day, day of week), social environment (the relationships among the students and the teacher, behavior concerns, or management plans already in place), and institutional mandates (pacing guides, required curriculum, standardized tests) that may impact or shape your teaching practices.

CTE STEP 5: ANALYZING THE LESSON

Although few people enjoy seeing themselves on video, dismiss your appearance and the sound of your voice and instead focus your attention on student learning, delivery of instruction, and classroom management. In this section, you are expected to critique your work; identify specific components of your lesson that were effective and those that were ineffective; consider instructional choices and management issues; and explain your analysis. What made one part of the lesson dynamic and another part problematic? Even if you think your CTE lesson is the best lesson you have ever taught, there is always room for growth. Prove to Joe and Josephine Assessor that you possess a wealth of knowledge related to instructional strategies and management techniques. If your lesson did not go as planned, admit that your ideas on paper did not translate into the desired actions or produce the intended results. Identify areas of concern, explain why there is room for improvement, and make recommendations for alternative strategies to demonstrate your understanding of effective teaching practices. Recall from *Chapter 4: Preparing your CalTPA Responses: Important Tips and Reminders* that reflection requires you to use analytical writing to present explanations, connections, and compelling argumentation instead of simple description.

In Step 5 you are asked to analyze student learning for the whole class and both focus students. You are also required to submit assessment samples for the two focus students, along with three other focus students of your choice. Samples that demonstrate high, medium, and low quality work for your additional three focus students are recommended to show a range in student achievement. Regardless of what assessment source you decide to use for your CTE lesson, it must be something you can actually submit for the assessors to review. In other words, you cannot state that you are going to assess individual students' responses to questions during the lesson unless you have a way to track each response. However, this does not mean that your tool has to be limited to a paper-and-pencil assessment with multiple choice or fill in the blank activities. You can also take digital photos of student projects and attach a rubric. Checklists can also be used for oral assessments, performances, or presentations. You might also want to refer back to *Chapter 9: Assessing Learning* to review tips related to organization and analysis of assessment data for the entire class. You should be prepared to give certain examples from the assessment data and video analysis to support your answers on parts A, B, and C under Step 5.

CTE STEP 6: REFLECTION AFTER INSTRUCTION

The last CTE step has only three questions that allow you to demonstrate that you understand how all of the pieces fit together. Remember that the rubric calls for *purposefully connected* responses that are *reinforced* throughout the task. Consider the following questions when formulating your responses.

1. Based on your analysis of student learning in this lesson, what are you going to teach next? Do you need to reteach anything in your lesson today or can you use the content in this lesson to build on the next concept? Remember, the assessment results should inform your instructional decisions.

2. What have you learned about planning instruction as a result of this experience? Why is it important to consider individual needs and use multiple strategies and resources when planning? Think about how your focus students' experience would have been different if you did not adapt strategies or materials. Or, consider how the experience would have been different for all learners if you did not include active teaching strategies or a variety of resources and activities.

3. What are your goals for continued growth in this profession? Provide specific examples of short-term and long-term goals. Are there organizations that offer yearly professional development opportunities or regional conferences related to your content area?

Conduct an Internet search on your own or check out the following organizations to learn more about content specific opportunities for professional development and leadership:

- National Council of Teachers of Mathematics *www.nctm.org*
- National Council for Social Studies *www.socialstudies.org/*
- National Science Teachers Association *www.nsta.org*
- National Council of Teachers of English *www.ncte.org*
- American Alliance for Health, Physical Education, Recreation, and Dance *www.aahperd.org*
- American Council on the Teaching of Foreign Languages *www.actfl .org*
- National Art Education Association *www.naea-reston.org*
- National Board for Professional Teaching Standards *http://www .nbpts.org/*

Focus on your professional growth by completing *You Try It! Gaze into the Crystal Ball.*

You Try It!

Gaze into the Crystal Ball

Imagine yourself teaching one year from now; five years; ten years; twenty-five years. What do you look like at each stage of your professional development? What do you need to do to ensure continuous growth and lifelong learning in this profession? Write three professional goals and put a projected date of accomplishment. Visualize your goals and aspirations now and always remember to provide a space for your continued growth throughout your career.

Goal #1. _____

Projected Date: _____

Goal #2. _____

Projected Date: _____

Goal #3. _____

Projected Date: _____

Chapter Summary

The Culminating Teaching Experience task provides you with the opportunity to connect your knowledge and skills through one lesson from beginning to end. All of the experiences and practice up to this point prepared you for success with this task. We hope you see the value from repeated practice and exercises that build on one another with varying degrees of difficulty. We know that practice in a variety of contexts with different levels of complexity has academic value and develops intellectual skills beyond basic recall or comprehension.

PONDER THIS . . .

How did your overall experience with the CalTPA affect your growth and development in the profession?

APPENDIX

(Sample Answers for *You Try It!* Activities)

INTRODUCTION

Here's What I'm Thinking So Far CalTPA Quiz (p. 5)

1. F: Although it is true that NCLB has provisions for well-prepared teachers, California state law, not federal law, mandates Teaching Performance Assessments (such as the CalTPA).
2. F: The CalTPA is a performance assessment—not an objective exam—and it is required to be embedded throughout the credential program.
3. F: Such a picky question! It measures 12 of 13 TPEs. TPE 12 (Professional, Legal, and Ethical Obligations) is measured elsewhere in your credential program.
4. T: The four are: Subject Specific Pedagogy, Designing Instruction, Assessing Learning, and Culminating Teaching Experience
5. T: Check with your program for specific procedures for re-taking the assessment.

Say This . . . Not That (p. 7)

1. Teacher B
2. Teacher D
3. Teacher E
4. Teacher H
5. Teacher J

CHAPTER 1: UNDERSTANDING THE CALTPA RUBRICS

Fill in the Blanks (p. 12)

Score Level 4	Score Level 3	Score Level 2	Score Level 1
The response provides evidence that **clearly, consistently, and convincingly** demonstrates evidence that . . . *[statement of outcomes demonstrated].*	The response provides evidence that **clearly** demonstrates evidence that . . . *[statement of outcomes demonstrated].*	The response provides evidence that **partially** demonstrates evidence that . . . *[statement of outcomes demonstrated].*	The response provides evidence that **does little or nothing to** demonstrate evidence that . . . *[statement of outcomes demonstrated].*
The preponderance of evidence provided for each of the following domains is **appropriate, relevant, accurate, and clear or detailed.**	The preponderance of evidence provided for each of the following domains is **appropriate, relevant, or accurate.**	The preponderance of evidence provided for each of the following domains is **minimal, limited, cursory, inconsistent, and/or ambiguous.**	The preponderance of evidence provided for each of the following domains is **inappropriate, irrelevant, inaccurate, or missing.**

Score Level 4	Score Level 3	Score Level 2	Score Level 1
Evidence is **purposefully connected and reinforced across the response.**	Evidence is **connected across the response.**	Evidence is **weakly connected across the response and may be inconsistent.**	Evidence is **unconnected across the response.**

Keep Your Story Straight (p. 14)

Step 1: C (Your one lesson on mean, median, mode, and range fits into this general topic.)

Step 2: D (This is the only response that accounts for the information given in the scenario.)

Step 3: B (This evidence addresses the standard specifically and for individual students. Note: Choosing N/A is virtually never appropriate for the CalTPA and would receive Score Level 1.)

Step 5: D (The other choices do not specifically connect to the prompt or the information in the scenario.)

CHAPTER 2: UNDERSTANDING CALTPA VOCABULARY

CalTPA Vocabulary Self-Rating (p. 18)

Although most terms are used more than once, check the chapters for where the terms are introduced.	
Term	**Chapter**
1. 504 Plan	6
2. Academic English	5
3. (Academic) language abilities	6
4. Accommodation	6
5. Adaptation	6
6. Attention-deficit hyperactivity disorder (ADHD)	6
7. Assessment type	7
8. Asthma	7
9. CalTPA	Intro
10. Candidate	Intro
11. Case study	7
12. California English Language Development Test (CELDT)	5
13. Comprehensible input	5

Term	Chapter
14. Content standards	Intro
15. Culture	5
16. Developmental needs	7
17. Diagnostic	7
18. Domain	1
19. English learner (EL)	5
20. English Language Development (ELD) Standards	5
21. Feedback strategies	7
22. Focus student	5
23. Formal assessment	7
24. Formative assessment	7
25. Frameworks	Intro
26. Gifted and Talented Education (GATE)	3
27. General education	7
28. Holistic	Intro
29. Individuals with Disability Education Act (IDEA)	6
30. Implementation	7
31. Individualized Education Program (IEP)	6
32. Induction	Intro
33. Informal assessment	7
34. Instructional resources	7
35. Instructional strategies	7
36. Learning environment	10
37. Learning experience	7
38. Learning goals	7
39. Lesson	7
40. Linguistic background	4
41. Misconceptions	5
42. Modification	6
43. Multiple measures	7
44. Performance assessment	Intro
45. Progress monitoring	7

46. Purpose	7
47. Rationale	6
48. Record of Evidence (ROE)	Intro
49. Reflection	7
50. Resource Specialist Program (RSP)	7
51. Rubric	1
52. Special education	6
53. Specially designed content instruction	5
54. Specific learning disabilities (or disorders)	7
55. Specific learning need	7
56. Speech and language disorders	6
57. Student activities	7
58. Student grouping	11
59. Summative assessment	Intro
60. Teaching Performance Expectation (TPE)	Intro
61. Unit	7
62. Universal Design for Learning	6

You Complete Me! (p. 22)

Word Connector Bank	
a. is an example of	d. is a component of
b. is a contrast to	e. is a synonym for
c. is the general category for	f. has nothing to do with
(Note: A true CalTPA wordsmith can probably justify other relationships as well. Other answers—except f—may also be accurate.)	

1. Lesson __d__ unit
2. Specific learning disability __a__ specific learning need
3. Special education __b__ general education
4. Formative assessment __b__ summative assessment
5. Comprehensible input __d__ specially designed content instruction
6. Adaptation __c__ accommodation
7. Specially designed content instruction __b__ English Language Development
8. Designing Instruction __d__ CalTPA
9. Performance assessment __a__ multiple measure
10. Lesson __e__ learning experience

CHAPTER 3: CHOOSING APPROPRIATE FOCUS STUDENTS

Focus Student Criteria (p. 28)

Student	Appropriate as focus student? (Circle Yes or No)	If yes, which task? (Circle one or more)	If yes, which focus student? Circle FS1 (EL) or FS2 (other)
1. José	Yes	DI AL CTE	FS1
2. Mary (Mary probably will not need adaptations for the lesson or assessment.)	No		
3. Halima	Yes	DI AL CTE	FS2
4. Brett (Brett does not need an adaptation for the lesson, so he will not be an appropriate choice. You'd need to change the lesson if you wanted to include Brett as FS2.)	No		
5. Miguel (Miguel probably is not appropriate for AL because AL requires an assessment rather than a lesson.)	Yes	DI CTE	FS2
6. Sarah (Sarah would not be appropriate for AL because AL requires an assessment rather than a lesson.)	Yes	DI CTE	FS2
7. Jenny (Jenny is not an appropriate FS for AL because there is no formal plan in place for her.)	Yes	DI CTE	FS2
8. Phuong (You can provide this information to the assessor in your description of the student.)	Yes	DI AL CTE	FS1

CHAPTER 4: PREPARING YOUR CALTPA RESPONSES: IMPORTANT TIPS AND REMINDERS

Acceptable or Not? (p. 32)

1. N	**2.** A	**3.** N	**4.** N	**5.** A
6. N	**7.** N	**8.** A	**9.** A	**10.** N

Addressing the Prompt (p. 36)

Answer 2 addresses the prompt because the candidate stated the parts of the assessment that he would keep, the part that he would change, and the rationale for both. Also, response 2 addresses all four components given in the directions.

Get Specific (p. 39)

Some of my students are overweight.

- Fourteen (40%) of my students are overweight.
- Seven of those are obese.
- Of the remaining students, just ten report engaging in regular vigorous physical activity like sports.

Other students have food allergies.

- Five students have food allergies, ranging from mild to severe.
- The severe allergy is to peanuts.

My lessons will incorporate this information.

- I will avoid candy and other low-nutrition foods as rewards or props.
- I will ensure that all students are educated about food allergies, and we will avoid allergy foods in instruction and class activities.
- I will incorporate physical activity across the curriculum, as advocated by Marzano (2007).
- I will use sports and physical activities as examples in my math lessons.

If the Shoe Fits... (p. 39)

1. descriptive
2. analytic
3. Sample 2 is the more appropriate response because of its connection to the prompt.

Analytical or Descriptive? (p. 40)

1. A   2. A   3. D   4. D   5. A

Teacher as Artist (p. 41)

Choice B. As we say in the chapter, for a high-stakes assessment where clarity rules and ambiguity is to be avoided, abstract responses are far too open to interpretation and too many inferences might be drawn.

CHAPTER 5: MAKING ADAPTATIONS FOR ENGLISH LEARNERS

Appropriate Practices for English Learners: Thumbs Up or Down? (p. 52)

1. Pao The teacher needs to make the content comprehensible for someone new to English. Examples include photographs, primary language support, focus on key ideas, and repetition.	

2. Adela Partnering is often a good idea, but it's insufficient alone. One major problem with partnering in Adela's case is that she needs to hear native English models, and all students need the opportunity to work with a variety of peers. Also, partnering should never be the only adaptation a teacher makes for English learners.	👎
3. Cruz These adaptations make the content accessible (that's comprehensible input) *and* provide Cruz and other students with the opportunity to use their English (comprehensible output) in a meaning-based, partner talk, which reduces anxiety of speaking in front of the whole class.	👍

Survivor: Voting EL Adaptations off the Island (p. 56)

1. b (Oral interviews have more of a chance of probing for what students know about the content even if the form of a student's speech is not polished.)
2. c (Athough it's true that the lesson is accessible as written, English learners—and really all students—need to practice their English aloud.)
3. a (Each of the adaptations suggested has at least one good point. However, Choice A [rich input with primary language support] best meets Danh's needs as a literate Vietnamese speaker whose current major need appears to be access to the content. Tip: If you have only one adaptation to give for your English learner, do not have it be partnering. Partnering is a fine strategy, but by itself it signals a certain lack of imagination; the teacher seems to be saying that she or he can think of no way to improve the instruction for a student.)

CHAPTER 6: MAKING ADAPTATIONS FOR LEARNERS WITH SPECIAL NEEDS

Thumbs Up or Thumbs Down: Appropriate Adaptations for Learners with Special Needs (p. 69)

1. 👍: The graphic organizer will assist Tessa in staying on task during the lecture. She will be able to recognize what is coming next in the lecture and to identify the important points. The teacher modeling with the larger version will also help her to recognize the important information and help her to take accurate notes. Having something to do during a lesson, rather than just listening, will help Tessa pay attention during the lesson.

2. 👍: Giving Trevor an alternative assignment that is based in real life and involves a non-routine problem will provide him with a challenge and will also allow him to demonstrate his knowledge in a way that is more appropriate for his skill level. There is no reason to make Trevor complete the textbook work that he has already mastered. Providing him with an alternative assignment that extends and expands on his knowledge will provide him with a more meaningful experience.

3. 👎: Keeping a student in at recess or break is a questionable practice to begin with. Punishing a student for being a slow worker is inappropriate indeed.

4. 👎: Moving Juan closer does not address his need to understand the vocabulary.

5. 👍: The word wall will give Ella a visual cue to look at and refer to. The realia will help reinforce the vocabulary in a tangible, real-life context. Multiple approaches like using a picture walk to introduce the story, reading to the class, and using the story map will support Ella in developing comprehension. Creating the story map together as a class will ensure that Ella is able to be successful in the project and will benefit her by allowing her to hear other students' responses.

6. 👎: Extra work is not an appropriate challenge for a bright student. Using a Wesley as a tutor does not support him or address his educational needs.

7. 👍: Allowing Meggie to express herself in ways other than speaking will assess what she really knows and not her ability to speak.

8. 👍: Giving Dan more time and less pressure to process requests and find the information will allow him to be more accurately assessed on his organization and notebook.

9. 👎: Kara needs more support in the lecture and perhaps a different kind of instruction. The teacher really has made no adaptations here for Kara. Passing off the teaching of content to a GATE student is inappropriate for both Kara and the GATE student.

Providing a Clear Rationale (p. 71)

1. Answer C provides a clear detailed, and rationale.
2. Answer A provides a clear, detailed and appropriate rationale.

CHAPTER 7: SUBJECT SPECIFIC PEDAGOGY

What Do You Know about Content Standards? (p. 77)

1. **T** Find content standards online at the California Department of Education's website (http://www.cde.ca.gov/be/st/ss/). If your area doesn't have content standards, it might at least have a framework (which gives a blueprint for instruction for that content). Frameworks are also found at the U.S. Department of Education's website.

2. **F** Content standards fit together. Standards are not just lists of topics. For every subject area, the standards fit together in a hierarchical structure. Be sure you've studied the structure into which content standards fit. Ask yourself: How are the standards in this subject area organized? What are the big groupings? What comes before? What comes after?

3. **F** *Content standards are statements of outcomes.* They explain what students should know and be able to do as a result of instruction. Teachers provide instruction that helps students to get from Point A to Point B. We don't *assign standards*; we *teach to them.*

4. **T** Learning goals and objectives are based on standards but may not look identical to the standards because individual teachers integrate standards and lessons in different ways based on what's appropriate for their setting and their students.

5. **F** Content standards vary in terms of specificity. Some standards can be achieved in a single lesson; others take several lessons. It is often acceptable for a lesson to address just one chunk of a single content standard. It can be equally acceptable for a lesson to address more than one content standard.

6. **T** We assess students' understandings before, during, and after instruction to check their progress on mastering standards.

Charting the SSP (p. 78)

Partially Completed for the Single Subject Art SSP (Source: Single Subject Art SSP task; http://www.ctc.ca.gov/educator-prep/TPA-California-candidates.html)

	Case Study 1 Subject Specific and Developmentally Appropriate Pedagogy	**Case Study 2** Assessment Practices
Grade level Subject area	Middle school (general art class) Color Theory	High school Two-dimensional art
Context *What are the setting and goals?*	• Two 45-minute sessions • Apply artistic processes • Create original works of art using color theory • Mix primary colors to obtain the color wheel • Identify and use color scheme(s)	• Three-week unit • Responding to art using vocabulary • Discuss, analyze, and write about principles of design in their own work and in the environment
People *Who are the students?* *What are their needs?*	• Need to learn in different ways and revisit content • Many enjoy school and each other • Much afterschool involvement • Most plan to attend two-year college • Need learning strategies • Need group skills • Support academic risk-taking	• Teacher is dissatisfied with the assessment plan and wants additional information on student understanding and misconceptions. • From the teacher's guide. It includes a diagnostic test, two quizzes, and a final test, all of which came from the teacher's guide. • Additional assessment: group critique and landscape painting
Job *In one sentence, what are you asked to do?*	Write a two-day lesson that addresses learning goals and student needs, then say why it's appropriate.	Analyze the assessment plan, incorporate additional assessment, analyze the use of additional assessment.

Prompts *(How many? What are they, briefly?)*	1. What's the plan? 2. Why is it appropriate (for this class, for their developmental needs, for making progress toward content standards)?	1. Give a strength and a weakness. 2. Explain how to incorporate additional assessment (7 prompts). 3. Say why use of additional assessment improves the assessment plan specific information to be gained.

Lesson Sort (p. 81)

Instructional Strategies	Student Activity
b. Show a fluid model of jumping a self-turned rope.	d. Watch a fluid model of jumping a self-turned rope.
e. Lead a discussion about what the class notices about the fluid model of jumping rope.	j. Participate in a discussion about the critical attributes of the fluid model of jumping rope.
h. Demonstrate the steps of jumping rope.	g. Watch the demonstration of the steps of jumping rope.
i. Distribute jump ropes to partners and monitor as they apply the steps of jumping rope.	f. Apply the steps for jumping rope by jumping rope.
c. Bring the class together and provide feedback on their progress. Ask for their next jump roping goals.	a. Listen to feedback about progress to date. Give a personal goal for jump roping.

Odd Man Out (p. 82)

Set One: Instructional Strategies

a. **ODD MAN OUT.** Round robin reading is rarely appropriate, and it doesn't meet any of the interests or needs stated for the class. It's also difficult to see its connection to learning goals.

b. Inferential thinking is appropriate for science class, and it's more likely to stretch this class of advanced learners than a simple identification activity.

c. This directly addresses the lesson goal and students' need to work together and learn time management.

Set Two: Student Activities

a. This addresses the lesson goal, students' preference for hands-on activities, and their limited Internet access at home.

b. **ODD MAN OUT.** This does not explicitly address any of the stated student interests or needs, and it's not explicitly connected to the learning goal (we don't know what the pages say).

c. This addresses the students needs of structured cooperative learning and the lesson goal of writing.

Looking for Links (p. 86)

Learning Goal	Assessment Type
1. Students will perform character-based monologues, using voice, blocking, and gesture.	Essay test scored with a rubric **The teacher should watch the students perform monologues.**
2. Students will safely use hand and power tools, machines, and equipment.	Observation with check list **Performance observation is indeed appropriate here, given the verb "use."**
3. Students will count by 2s, 5s, and 10s to 100.	Oral test (coins allowed as manipulatives) **Oral counting with support from manipulatives directly address the goal.**
4. Students will use simple and compound sentences in speaking.	Multiple choice quiz **The goal specifies "in speaking."**
5. Students in Spanish class will correctly conjugate regular verbs in the preterite tense (one form of past tense).	Vocabulary test (Students write the vocabulary terms they hear while listening to a recording of a native Spanish speaker.) **Writing vocabulary terms is a different goal than conjugating verbs.**
6. Chemistry students know how to use Le Chatelier's principle to predict the effect of changes in concentration, temperature, and pressure.	Short-answer test with realistic problems related to changes in concentration, temperature, and pressure. **Students' knowledge of how to use the principle can in fact be checked by asking them to use it to solve relevant problems.**

Sort It Out! (p. 88)

Timing	Diagnostic	i. Informal Reading Inventory
	Formative	b. Wipe boards c. Chapter quizzes e. Reflective journals
	Summative	a. Standardized tests d. Essays f. Multimedia presentations (e.g., PowerPoint, podcasts)

| Formality | Informal | b. Wipe boards
e. Reflective journals
i. Informal reading inventory |
| | Formal | a. Standardized tests
c. Chapter quizzes
d. Essays
f. Multimedia presentations
(e.g., PowerPoint, podcasts)
(if conditions are highly specified) |

There's Gotta Be a Better Way! (p. 91)

| 1. The teacher presents a textbook-driven lecture on 15 major points. Students take notes, then pack up when the bell rings and leave. | • Start by posting and discussing lesson outcomes.
• Focus on fewer points.
• Include connections to the students' home culture, straying from the text to find them.
• Include real objects, photographs, or audio and video clips.
• Make speech comprehensible by slowing down, using repetition, using gestures, and minimizing figures of speech.
• Use preview/review.
• Check for understanding throughout with white boards.
• Provide primary language support for a couple of key abstract concepts.
• To scaffold, provide skeleton notes.
• Use 10/2 processing.
• Practice the information through structured peer interaction. Some choices: "Turn to your neighbor…"; think-pair-share; numbered heads together; seasonal partners.
• Close by reviewing major ideas, which are posted. |
| 2. To synthesize what they have learned, the students write 45-minute independent in-class essays on causes of the Great Depression. | • Extended responses and some writing are appropriate for intermediate English learners, but scaffolding is important.
• Use word banks, perhaps including some student-generated terms.
• Prewrite as a class, focusing on structure (such as frames).
• Rehearse with peers before writing. Ideas include seasonal partners, think-pair-share.
• Consider alternate forms of writing that embed language in rich contexts. One example is dialogue journals.
• Allow students to include drawings in their writing.
• Consider an oral interview with the teacher before, instead of, or in addition to the written essay. |

3. During a whole-class discussion, students who raise their hands contribute individual interpretations with supporting details on their concept of "loneliness."	• Ensure understanding of the abstract term before discussion. Use and discuss images or video clips, primary-language explanations, and enactments of the term. • Allow for structured peer interaction (for rehearsal) before the discussion. Try "turn to your neighbor" or seasonal partners. • Use wait time. • After rehearsal in small groups, require all students (not just fluent English speakers) to contribute an idea, with the length of contribution appropriate for EL level. • In responding to student comments, focus on meaning and not on error correction or form. Model correct sentence structure and pronunciation.
4. Before the lesson, the teacher presents a list of ten vocabulary terms and students work in pairs to look up and record definitions in their individual journals.	• Use fewer terms (only 3 to 5 per lesson). • Only preteach those that are required for success in the lesson. Teach the remaining terms in context during the lesson. • Practicing dictionary skills is a good idea, but it shouldn't be the sole focus of vocabulary learning. Instead act out the words; draw pictures; teach word parts; give antonyms, synonyms, and cognates; use context and examples to develop word meanings.

DWIT . . . Or Not! (p. 95)

Scenario	DWIT suggestion violated
a. Modify the assessment for the student; don't just delete it.	5
b. Social skills are predictably difficult for highly gifted students, particularly before age 9. Pick out some social skills and teach them. Your student needs strategies to make and keep friends at his developmental level.	3
c. A short stature is only one thing your student possesses. He still can thrive in cooperative and competitive settings and can benefit from learning basket ball and from the aerobic exercise and social lessons that come from basketball.	2
d. Students on the autism spectrum most frequently struggle with environmental stimulation and changes.	1
e. Yes, expectations need to be high, but instructional modifications are also required for students to meet those expectations. This student needs help in incrementally building skills that will allow her to organize her notebook.	4

CHAPTER 8: DESIGNING INSTRUCTION
CalTPA DI Warm Up (p. 98)

1. DI
2. Step 1: Academic Content Selection and Learning about Students; Step 2: Learn About Two Focus Students; Step 3: Plan for the Whole Class; Step 4: Plan Lesson Adaptations for Two Focus Students; Step Five: Reflect.
3. SSP and DI
4. DI

---

1. Academic Content Selection and Learning about Students
2. Linguistic background, academic language abilities, content knowledge, and skills, physical, social and emotional development, cultural and health considerations, interests and aspirations
3. English learner and a student with a different instructional challenge
4. Standards, unit of study and learning goals
5. No
6. Plan a lesson for the whole class based on what you know about the students. Provide a rationale for your planning decisions.
7. Describe your decision about lesson adaptations and a rationale for those decisions
8. What information collected about students most influenced your instruction and how will you connect student characteristics to instructional planning in the future.

Details, Details! (p. 101)

1. B is the more detailed and appropriate response.
2. A is a more detailed and relevant response.

Active Participation (p. 103)

1. Use seasonal partners to compare answers, switching partners between problems; have students meet in small groups to solve one of five problems, then check with others in other groups for the remaining four problems; assign partners to solve problems on the board, an overhead, or the interactive white board, and then compare answers. Ask students to analyze work for sticky points to begin the lesson.
2. Call on five students. Use think-pair-share. Use partner talk. Use wipe boards. Do quick writes.
3. Use choral reading, partner reading, or silent reading, and allow students who struggle with reading to listen to a recording simultaneously.
4. Use choral response; use hand signals; have partners compare answers; pull cards or sticks; ask for contrasting or connecting responses.

Brush Up on Your Adaptations (p. 106)

1. The first part of this lesson that Rosie will probably have difficulty with is reading the historic letter. The teacher can easily adapt

for this by projecting the historic letter for all to see and reading it aloud to the class. Rosie will have difficulty taking notes. For this, the teacher could provide her with a strategic note-taking guide, so that she simply has to fill in one or two words for each prompt in order to record the information. Lastly, Rosie could be allowed to word process her response and complete her journal entry on the computer. This will allow her to express what she knows without being restricted by her inability to write neatly.

2. Asad will have difficulty with the academic language involved in the lesson. Asad would benefit from being frontloaded with vocabulary relevant to the lesson. The teacher could introduce the vocabulary before the lesson using realia to engage the students. Asad, as well as the other students, could record new vocabulary in a Cognitive Content Dictionary, including what they think the word means, the actual meaning, and a picture to remind them of the meaning. Asad can refer back to this Cognitive Content Dictionary as needed.

3. Andrew already knows the material in the textbook and will therefore need a challenge. One solution is to give Andrew an alternative assignment. The teacher could model for him a real-life example of GCF, such as: "Sarah is making identical balloon arrangements for a surprise party. She has 32 blue balloons, 24 white balloons, and 16 yellow balloons. Sarah wants each balloon arrangement to have the same number of each color. If every balloon is used, what is the greatest number of arrangements that she can make?" After Andrew solves the problem, the teacher could ask him to come up with his own similar problem to demonstrate GCF. Giving Andrew an alternative assignment will challenge his thinking and expand on what he already knows. There is no need to have him also complete the textbook work.

CHAPTER 9: ASSESSING LEARNING

I Spy (p. 110)

Same as Designing Instruction	Different from Designing Instruction
• Pick content area and standards • Learn about the whole class • Pick and learn about two focus students • Plan a class activity • Modify it for focus students • Reflect	• Class activity is an assessment, not a lesson • Focus student 2 must have a formal plan (IEP or 504) • Must actually deliver the assessment • Pick up student samples and score them

Is that Your Final Answer? (p. 116)

Case Study One

Identify the difficulty the student may have with this assessment.	What specific information from the case study led you to this conclusion?	Suggest an adaptation.	Provide a rationale for the adaptation.
Completing the chart.	She has dsygraphia, which makes her handwriting difficult to read. She also loses her place when she looks away from the paper on which she is writing.	I would assess Lilly through verbal interaction. I would show her the picture and ask her the questions. She could dictate her answers to me and I could write them on the chart for her or she could record her responses using a recorder.	Having Lilly respond to the prompts orally will allow her to demonstrate what she knows about the topic without having to write. In this way I can bypass the dysgraphia issue. Also, looking from the picture to the paper she records her answers on would be difficult for Lilly and she might lose her place. Once again, having her answer the questions aloud and not having her write will allow her to focus on the picture and not have to shift from the paper to the picture and back again.

Case Study Two

Identify the difficulty the student may have with this assessment.	What specific information from the case study led you to this conclusion?	Suggest an adaptation.	Provide a rationale for the adaptation.
Answering the two written questions.	CELDT results place him as an Early Intermediate level English learner. His oral proficiency and comprehension are much better than his writing skills.	I will have Pablo record his ideas with a tape recorder. I will also have Pablo draw pictures of the dangers that people may have faced along the way. I will ask him to explain his pictures to me orally.	He can answer both questions aloud and I will be able to assess him without his writing difficulties interfering. The pictures may help him generate his thoughts for the questions and again allow him to bypass the writing aspect of the assessment.

Case Study Three

Identify the difficulty the student may have with this assessment.	What specific information from the case study led you to this conclusion?	Suggest an adaptation.	Provide a rationale for the adaptation.
Oral assessment.	Emily has a speech impediment. It is difficult for her to say certain sounds such as *r* and *l*. Because of this, Emily often chooses not to respond verbally, even in a one-to-one situation.	I will ask her questions that would allow her to point or gesture. Here are some of the prompts I might use: "Point to something that is a circle." "Point to something that is a square." Instead of asking Emily to identify whether objects are rectangles or squares, I could give her a variety of different objects and ask her to sort them into groups according to their shape, for example, squares in one group and rectangles in another. I could then give her labels with the word for each shape written on them and ask her to place the correct label above each group she sorted.	Emily may not speak if I try to assess her orally. By asking her to point or gesture or sort, I will assess what Emily knows without having her speech impediment and reluctance to speak interfere with the assessment.

Survey Says… Analyzing Responses (p. 119)

Some Possible Trends:

1. Andi needs additional support with the learning objectives measured on this assessment. She scored 20% on the quiz. She answered 1 out of 5 questions correctly.
2. Lynda needs support with the learning objectives related to questions 4 and 5. She scored 60% on the quiz. She answered 3 out of 5 questions correctly.
3. All five students mastered the learning objectives for question 1.
4. Three out of five students need additional support with the learning objectives associated with questions 4 and 5.

CHAPTER 10: CULMINATING TEACHING EXPERIENCE

Pass on the Popcorn (p. 124)

Some Alternatives to Popcorn Reading

- Choral reading (Students read text aloud together.)
- Partner reading (Two students read text aloud together, or take turns. They sit ear-to-ear.)
- Cloze reading (Teacher reads the majority of the text aloud and students follow along silently. Every few words, the teacher omits a relevant vocabulary word and students fill in the blank aloud.)
- Reader's theater (Students use scripts or prepare them themselves. They choose their parts and rehearse repeatedly before reading as a performance.)
- Mumble reading (Students read text aloud under their breath and at their own pace.)

How Not to Teach (p. 125)

Problem areas:
- Does not use an effective hook to engage students.
- Does not ensure active and equitable participation by all students.
- Does not take students' interests or learning styles into account
- Does not differentiate instruction
- Does not facilitate discussion.
- Does not take students' prior knowledge into account.
- Students are passive receivers of knowledge.
- Only emphasizes basic knowledge and comprehension of text.
- Limited resources: The textbook only provides a narrow and often conservative perspective.

Strategies: (not pedagogically sound)
- Asking questions
- Looking for the "correct" answer according to one perspective.
- Round Robin Reading
- Reading the textbook in an uninteresting way
- Assigning vocabulary words without meaning, rich development
- Assigning chapter review

Recommendations for improvement:
- Conduct a simulation
- Photo analysis
- True/false sorts
- Explore primary source documents
- Use vocabulary knowledge ratings to find out what students already know
- Conduct historical inquiry
- Explore multiple resources and perspectives
- Pull name sticks to ensure active and equitable participation
- Accept more than one answer to a question
- Ask questions that promote a higher-level of thinking

Gaze into the Crystal Ball (p. 134)

Examples of professional goals:

1. Join a national professional organization.
2. Pursue an advanced degree.
3. Pursue National Board certification.
4. Attend conferences.
5. Present at conferences.
6. Subscribe to peer-reviewed journals.
7. Serve as department chair or grade level chair, or serve on another school-based committee.
8. Attend workshops to improve instruction.
9. Conduct action research in your classroom.
10. Join the online professional community through blogs, networking sites (Classroom 2.0), and other venues.
11. Develop a family outreach program for your school.

REFERENCES

Brown, T. (2006). Attention deficit disorder: The unfocused mind in children and adults. New Haven, CT: Yale University Press.

California Commission on Teacher Credentialing. (2003). California's teaching performance expectations. Retrieved from www.ctc.ca.gov/educator-prep/TPA-files/TPEs-Full-Version.pdf.

California Commission on Teacher Credentialing. (2009). CalTPA California teaching performance assessment candidate handbook. Retrieved from http://www.ctc.ca.gov/educator-prep/TPA-files/CandidateHandbook.pdf.

California Department of Education (2006). English learners in California frequently asked questions. Retrieved from http://www.cde.ca.gov/sp/el/er/documents/elfaq.doc.

Center for Applied Special Technology CAST (2010). What is universal design for learning? Retrieved from http://www.cast.org/research/udl/index.

Center for Research on Education, Diversity & Excellence (2002). The five standards for effective pedagogy. Retrieved from http://crede.berkeley.edu/research/crede/standards.html.

Children and Adults with Attention Deficit Hyperactivity Disorder (2009). Understanding AD/HD. Retrieved from http://www.chadd.org/AM/.Template.cfm?Section=Understanding

Covert, B. (2009). Descriptive writing. Retrieved from http://edhelper.com/ReadingComprehension_33_35.html.

Cummins, J. (1981). The role of primary language development in promoting educational success for language minority students. In California State Department of Education (Ed.), Schooling and language minority students: A theoretical framework. (pp. 3–49). Los Angeles: National Dissemination and Assessment Center.

Echevarria, J., Vogt, M. E. & Short, D. (2010a). Making content comprehensible for elementary English learners: The SIOP Model. Boston: Allyn & Bacon.

Echevarria, J., Vogt, M. E. & Short, D. (2010b). Making content comprehensible for secondary English learners: The SIOP Model. Boston: Allyn & Bacon.

Fillmore, L. W., & Snow, K. (2000). What teachers need to know about language. ERIC Clearinghouse on Languages and Linguistics Special Report. Retrieved from http://citeseerx.ist.psu.edu/viewdoc/download?doi=10.1.1.92.9117&rep=rep1&type=pdf

Gersten, R., Baker, S. K., Shanahan, T., Linan-Thompson, S., Collins, P., & Scarcella, R. (2007). Effective literacy and English language instruction for English learners in the elementary grades: A practice guide (NCEE 2007-4011). Washington, DC: National Center for Education Evaluation and Regional Assistance, Institute of Education Sciences, U.S. Department of Education. Retrieved from http://ies.ed.gov/ncee/wwc/publications/practiceguides.

Glasser, W. (1986). Control theory in the classroom. New York: Harper and Row.

Guillaume, A. (2008). K-12 Classroom teaching: A primer for New Professionals. Upper Saddle River, NJ: Prentice Hall.

Hill, J. D., & Flynn, K. M. (2006). Classroom instruction that works with English learners. Alexandria, VA: Association for Supervision and Curriculum Development.

Krashen, S. D. (1981). Second language acquisition and second language learning. Pergamom Press. Retrieved from http://www.sdkrashen.com/SL_Acquisition_and_Learning/index.html.

Learning Disabilities Association of America (2006). Retrieved from http://www.ldanatl.org/.

Marzano, R. J. (2007). The art and science of teaching: A comprehensive framework for effective instruction. Alexandria, VA: ASCD.

Meyer, L. M. (2000). Barriers to meaningful instruction for English learners. Theory Into Practice, 39, 228–236.

National Association of Parents with Children in Special Education (2007). Speech and language impairments. Retrieved from http://www.napcse.org/exceptionalchildren/speechandlanguageimpairments.php.

National Center for Education Statistics (NCES) (2009). Retrieved from http://nces.ed.gov/fastfacts/display.asp?id=64.

National Center for Education Statistics (NCES) (2010). Public elementary and secondary school student enrollment and staff counts from the Common Core of Data: School Year 2007–08 First Look. Retrieved from http://nces.ed.gov/pubs2010/2010309.pdf.

National Center on Response to Intervention (2010). Retrieved from http://www.rti4success.org/index.php?option=com_frontpage&Itemid=1.

National Center on Student Progress Monitoring (2009). Retrieved from http://www.studentprogress.org/.

National Education Association (1975). Code of ethics. Retrieved from http://www.nea.org/home/30442.htm.

National Resource Center for ADHD (2008). The disorder named ADHD. Retrieved from http://www.help4adhd.org/en/about/what/WWK1.

Pennington, M. (2009, September 30). Why round robin and popcorn reading are evil (Web blog). Retrieved from http://penningtonpublishing.com/blog/reading/why-round-robin-and-popcorn-reading-are-evil/.

Reid, S., Kiefer, K., Barnes, L., & Kowalski, D. (2010). Writing guide: Audience. Retrieved from http://writing.colostate.edu/guides/processes/audmod/.

Salend, S. (2010). Creating inclusive classrooms: Reflective and effective practices. 7th. ed. Upper Saddle River, New Jersey: Prentice Hall.

Spencer, B. H., & Guillaume, A. M. (2009). 35 strategies for content area vocabulary. Upper Saddle River, NJ: Pearson Merrill Prentice Hall.

Strunk, W., & White, E. B., (2008). The elements of style. 50th ed. New York: Longman.

Swain, M. (1985). Communicative competence: Some roles of comprehensible input and comprehensible output in its development. In S. Gass & C. Madden (Eds)., Input in second language acquisition. Rowley, MA: Newbury House. (pp. 235–253).

Thomas, W. P., & Collier, V. P. (2001). A national study of school effectiveness for language minority students' long-term academic achievement final report: Project 1.1. Retrieved from http://crede.berkeley.edu/research/llaa/1.1_final.html.

U.S. Department of Education (2004a). Public Law Print of PL 107-110, the No Child Left Behind Act of 2001. Retrieved from http://www2.ed.gov/policy/elsec/leg/esea02/index.html

U.S. Department of Education (2004b). Public Law Print of PL 108-446, The Individuals with Disabilities Education Improvement Act of 2004. Retrieved from http://idea.ed.gov/download/statute.html.

U.S. Department of Education (2007). Q and A: Questions and answers on Response to Intervention (RTI) and Early Intervening Services (EIS). Retrieved from http://idea.ed.gov/explore/view/p/,root,dynamic,QaCorner,8.

U.S. Department of Health and Human Services (2006). Your rights under Section 504 of the Rehabilitation Act Fact Sheet. Retrieved from http://www.hhs.gov/ocr/504.html.

U.S. Department of Justice (2005). A guide to disabilities rights and laws—Americans with Disabilities Act. Retrieved from http://www.ada.gov/cguide.htm.

U.S. Department of Justice (2010). Americans with Disabilities Act. Retrieved from http://www.ada.gov.

Vaughn, S., Bos, C., & Schumm, J. (2010). Teaching students who are exceptional, diverse, and at risk in the general education classroom. 5th. ed. Upper Saddle River, New Jersey: Prentice Hall.

Watanabe, T. (2010, May 28). Many English learners still struggle with the language, study shows. LA Times. Retrieved from http://articles.latimes.com/2010/may/28/local/la-me-0528-english-20100528.

Williams, L. (2009). *Learning disabilities part one: An introduction.* My Expert Solution. Retrieved from http://www.myexpertsolution.com/experts/lywilliams/articles/330946/.

Williams, L. (2009). Learning disabilities: Part two: What to do if you think your child has a learning disability. My Expert Solution.

INDEX